Ecuador Cookbook
Authentic Recipes

THE RICH AND DIVERSE FLAVORS OF ECUADORIAN CUISINE

TERESA P. MORENO

ECUADOR COOKBOOK
Uncover the Rich and Diverse Flavors of Ecuadorian Cuisine.

© Teresa P. Moreno
© E.G.P. Editorial
   ISBN-13: 9798322303411

Copyright © 2024
All rights reserved.

FLAVOURS THAT CROSS BORDERS

From my youngest days, narratives of Ecuador and the strains of traditional music were ever-present, crafting a strong bond with my cultural roots despite the geographical separation from my grandmother's native land. My grandmother, embodying resilience and optimism, together with my grandfather, decided in the 1950s to make New York their new abode, seeking improved futures for their descendants, and becoming part of the vibrant and varied Ecuadorian community in Queens.

The choice to navigate vast distances and make a home in a foreign territory was formidable; yet, my grandmother's fortitude and hopeful perspective were steadfast. Her tales infused me with the importance of maintaining our cultural and ancestral ties, particularly through culinary practices. My grandmother's kitchen turned into a sanctuary of scents and tastes, crafted not just for nourishment but as bridges to our Ecuadorian heritage.

My grandmother impressed upon me that culinary arts go beyond the simple preparation of meals; they are an expression of love, a way to cherish our heritage and share our narratives with the next generations. Each recipe she shared was steeped in a tale, a teaching, or a memory of Ecuador, turning every meal into a festivity of our identity.

The role of Ecuadorian cuisine in my life was profoundly influenced not just by my grandmother's teachings but also by literature that celebrated the richness and diversity of our culinary traditions. These works were crucial for my grandmother to perfect her recipes, which became central to our family gatherings in New York.

Now, as an adult and the author of this narrative, my goal is to safeguard and propagate my grandmother's culinary legacy. Though she has passed, her spirit and insights continue to guide me every time I prepare one of her recipes. This narrative is a homage to her, to her life filled with strength, love, and a passion for cooking, intending to inspire others to discover the unity and joy that cooking brings.

Through this narrative, I hope that readers will not only learn to craft genuine Ecuadorian dishes but will also understand the commitment and affection my grandmother poured into each recipe. May this book serve as a bridge between generations and cultures, illustrating that no matter where we are, culinary traditions can create a haven for both the heart and soul.

TABLE OF CONTENTS

BREAKFASTS 9
SOUPS 20
BROTHS 38
SEAFOOD DISHES 50
BEEF DISHES 64
PORK DISHES 77
CHICKEN DISHES 90
VEGETARIAN DISHES 105
RICE DISHES 118
SAUCES 133
BREADS 141
DESSERTS 152
RECIPE LIST 167

BREAKFASTS

Ecuadorian breakfasts stand apart in the realm of global cuisine, celebrated for their rich nutritional content and the unique use of indigenous ingredients. These morning meals are a tapestry of flavors and textures, often combining fresh fruits, grains, and proteins to kickstart the day with a balanced and energizing meal. This culinary tradition reflects not only the country's biodiverse landscape but also its cultural heritage, offering a delectable palette of tastes that nourish the body and soul.

The versatility of Ecuadorian breakfasts is unmatched, easily adapting to fit any dietary need or preference while never compromising on taste or nutritional value. Whether it's a light fare of fresh fruit and yogurt or a hearty serving of llapingachos (stuffed potato patties), the emphasis is always on wholesome, unprocessed ingredients. This approach ensures a plethora of vitamins, minerals, and other essential nutrients, making these meals a cornerstone of healthy eating.

Ecuadorian breakfasts thus serve as a vibrant introduction to the day, providing not just sustenance but a celebration of the nation's rich culinary traditions. They exemplify how food can be both delicious and nutritious, setting a benchmark for how we approach the first meal of the day.

BOLÓN DE VERDE

Ingredients

- Green plantains - 3 large.
- Cheddar cheese - 1 cup, grated.

- Bacon - 1/2 cup, cooked and crumbled.
- Salt - to taste.
- Butter - 1 tablespoon, for frying.

Instructions

1. Peel the plantains and boil them in water until soft.

2. Mash the plantains while warm and mix with the cheese and bacon.

3. Form the mixture into balls.

4. Heat the butter in a pan and fry the balls until golden brown on all sides.

TIGRILLO

Ingredients

- Green plantains - 2 large.
- Eggs - 2.
- Grated cheese - 1 cup.
- Salt and pepper - to taste.
- Olive oil - 2 tablespoons.

Instructions

1. Peel and grate the plantains.

2. In a skillet, heat the olive oil and add the grated plantains, cooking until they are soft.

3. Beat the eggs with salt and pepper, then add them to the skillet, mixing well.

4. Add the cheese and stir until it melts.

MOTE PILLO

Ingredients

- Hominy (mote) - 2 cups, cooked.
- Eggs - 4.
- Milk - 1/4 cup.
- Scallions - 1/4 cup, finely chopped.
- Salt and pepper - to taste.
- Butter - 2 tablespoons.

Instructions

1. In a pan, melt the butter and sauté the scallions until soft.

2. Add the hominy and cook for a few minutes, stirring occasionally.

3. Beat the eggs with milk, salt, and pepper, then pour over the hominy mixture.

4. Cook, stirring until the eggs are set.

EMPANADAS DE VIENTO

Ingredients

- All-purpose flour - 2 cups.
- Water - 1/2 cup.
- Butter - 1 tablespoon.
- Sugar - 1 teaspoon.
- Salt - 1/2 teaspoon.
- White cheese - 1 cup, crumbled.
- Oil - for frying.

Instructions

1. Mix the flour, water, butter, sugar, and salt to form a dough.

2. Divide the dough into small portions and roll out into circles.

3. Fill each circle with cheese, then fold and seal the edges.

4. Fry in hot oil until puffed and golden.

LLAPINGACHOS

Ingredients

- Potatoes - 3 cups, mashed.
- Annatto oil - 2 tablespoons.
- Spring onions - 1/4 cup, finely chopped.
- Salt - to taste.
- White cheese - 1 cup, grated.
- Oil - for frying.

Instructions

1. Mix the mashed potatoes with annatto oil, spring onions, salt, and cheese.

2. Form the mixture into small patties.

3. Heat oil in a pan and fry the patties until golden brown on both sides.

CEVICHE DE CAMARÓN (BREAKFAST VERSION)

Ingredients

- Shrimp - 2 cups, cooked and peeled.
- Lime juice - 1/2 cup.
- Tomato - 1 large, diced.
- Red onion - 1/4 cup, thinly sliced.
- Cilantro - 2 tablespoons, chopped.
- Salt and pepper - to taste.
- Orange juice - 1/4 cup.
- Ketchup - 2 tablespoons (optional).

Instructions

1. In a bowl, combine the shrimp with lime juice and let it marinate for about 10 minutes.

2. Add the tomato, red onion, cilantro, salt, and pepper. Mix well.

3. Stir in the orange juice and ketchup if using. Adjust the seasoning if necessary.

4. Refrigerate until ready to serve, ideally chilled for at least an hour.

HUMITAS

Ingredients

- Corn - 4 cups, kernels.
- Butter - 1/4 cup, melted.
- Eggs - 2.
- Sugar - 1/4 cup.
- Salt - 1 teaspoon.

- Corn flour - 1/2 cup.
- Cheese - 1 cup, grated.

Instructions

1. Blend the corn kernels until smooth.

2. Mix the blended corn with melted butter, eggs, sugar, salt, and corn flour.

3. Stir in the grated cheese.

4. Wrap the mixture in corn husks and steam for about 40 minutes.

QUIMBOLITOS

Ingredients

- Corn flour - 2 cups.
- Baking powder - 1 teaspoon.
- Sugar - 1 cup.
- Butter - 1/2 cup, melted.
- Eggs - 3.
- Milk - 1/2 cup.
- Raisins - 1/4 cup.

Instructions

1. Mix the corn flour, baking powder, and sugar in a bowl.

2. Add the melted butter, eggs, and milk. Mix until smooth.

3. Fold in the raisins.

4. Wrap the batter in banana leaves or aluminum foil and steam for about 25 minutes.

PAN DE YUCA

Ingredients

- Yuca flour - 2 cups.
- Cheese - 2 cups, grated.
- Eggs - 3.
- Baking powder - 1 teaspoon.
- Butter - 1 tablespoon, softened.
- Salt - 1/2 teaspoon.

Instructions

1. Preheat the oven to 350°F (175°C).

2. In a large bowl, mix together the yuca flour, cheese, eggs, baking powder, butter, and salt until a dough forms.

3. Roll the dough into small balls and place on a baking sheet.

4. Bake for 20-25 minutes, or until they are golden and puffed.

YAPINGACHOS

Ingredients

- Potatoes - 3 cups, boiled and mashed.
- Annatto (Achiote) oil - 2 tablespoons.
- Green onions - 1/4 cup, finely chopped.
- Salt - to taste.
- Cheese - 1 cup, grated.

- Oil - for frying.

Instructions

1. Mix the mashed potatoes with annatto oil, green onions, and salt.

2. Take a portion of the potato mixture, flatten it, and fill with cheese. Then, form it into a patty.

3. Heat oil in a pan and fry each patty until they are golden on both sides.

ENCEBOLLADO (MORNING AFTER SOUP OFTEN EATEN FOR BREAKFAST)

Ingredients

- Tuna - 2 cups, cooked and shredded.
- Yucca - 2 cups, boiled and cut into bite-size pieces.
- Red onions - 1 cup, thinly sliced.
- Tomatoes - 1 cup, chopped.
- Cilantro - 1/4 cup, chopped.
- Lime - 2, juiced.
- Water - 6 cups.
- Salt and pepper - to taste.

Instructions

1. In a large pot, bring the water to a boil and add the yucca. Cook until tender.

2. Add the cooked tuna, onions, tomatoes, cilantro, lime juice, salt, and pepper. Simmer for 20 minutes.

3. Serve hot, adjusted with salt and pepper to taste.

TAMAL DE MAÍZ

Ingredients

- Corn dough - 4 cups.
- Pork lard - 1/4 cup.
- Chicken broth - 1 cup.
- Onion - 1/2 cup, finely chopped.
- Garlic - 2 cloves, minced.
- Green peas - 1/2 cup.
- Carrots - 1/2 cup, diced.
- Salt and pepper - to taste.
- Banana leaves - for wrapping.

Instructions

1. Mix the corn dough with pork lard and chicken broth to get a smooth consistency.

2. Sauté the onion and garlic until they are translucent.

3. Mix the sautéed onion and garlic, green peas, and carrots into the corn dough. Season with salt and pepper.

4. Place a spoonful of the mixture on a banana leaf, fold it, and tie it with string.

5. Steam the tamales for about an hour or until the dough is cooked through.

MOROCHO

Ingredients

- Morocho corn - 1 cup, soaked overnight.
- Water - 6 cups.
- Milk - 4 cups.

- Sugar - 1 cup.
- Cinnamon sticks - 2.
- Cloves - 4.
- Raisins - 1/2 cup.
- Grated coconut - 1/2 cup.

Instructions

1. Rinse the morocho corn and cook in water with cinnamon sticks and cloves until soft.

2. Add milk, sugar, raisins, and grated coconut. Cook over low heat, stirring frequently, until the mixture thickens.

3. Serve warm, garnished with extra grated coconut if desired.

CHUCULA

Ingredients

- Bananas - 3, ripe and mashed.
- Milk - 2 cups.
- Cinnamon - 1 teaspoon.
- Cloves - 1/4 teaspoon.
- Sugar - to taste.

Instructions

1. In a blender, mix the mashed bananas, milk, cinnamon, cloves, and sugar until smooth.

2. Pour the mixture into a pot and cook over medium heat until it thickens, stirring constantly.

3. Serve hot or cold, as preferred.

AREPAS ECUATORIANAS

Ingredients

- Cornmeal - 2 cups.
- Warm water - 2 cups.
- Salt - 1 teaspoon.
- Cheese - 1 cup, grated.
- Butter - for frying.

Instructions

1. In a bowl, mix the cornmeal, warm water, and salt to form a dough.

2. Stir in the grated cheese until evenly distributed.

3. Form the dough into small balls, then flatten to form discs.

4. Heat butter in a pan and fry the arepas until golden on both sides.

SOUPS

Ecuadorian soups are a cornerstone of the country's culinary identity, renowned for their depth of flavor and nutritional richness. These comforting bowls are crafted from a diverse array of local ingredients, including fresh vegetables, legumes, and meats, all simmering together to create a harmonious blend of tastes and textures. This diversity not only showcases Ecuador's agricultural bounty but also highlights the cultural significance of soups in daily meals, emphasizing their role in bringing families together.

The adaptability of Ecuadorian soups is remarkable, catering to an extensive range of dietary preferences and nutritional needs without sacrificing flavor. From the hearty and meaty to the light and vegetarian, each recipe is a testament to the ingenuity of Ecuadorian cooking, seamlessly incorporating whole, nutrient-dense ingredients. This ensures that every spoonful is packed with essential vitamins and minerals, supporting overall health and well-being.

Thus, Ecuadorian soups epitomize the balance between mouthwatering flavors and healthful eating. They stand as a vibrant reminder of how traditional dishes can be both nourishing and a source of culinary delight, making them a cherished part of Ecuador's gastronomic legacy.

LOCRO DE PAPA

Ingredients

- Potatoes - 4 cups, diced.
- Avocado - 1, sliced for garnish.

- Cheese - 1 cup, grated.
- Milk - 1 cup.
- Onion - 1/2 cup, finely chopped.
- Garlic - 2 cloves, minced.
- Annatto oil - 2 tablespoons.
- Water or chicken broth - 4 cups.
- Salt and pepper - to taste.
- Cilantro - 1/4 cup, chopped for garnish.

Instructions

1. In a large pot, heat the annatto oil over medium heat. Add onions and garlic, sauté until soft.

2. Add the potatoes and cook for a few minutes, stirring frequently.

3. Pour in the water or chicken broth and bring to a boil. Reduce heat and simmer until the potatoes are tender.

4. Mash some of the potatoes in the pot to thicken the soup. Stir in the milk and cheese, and season with salt and pepper.

5. Serve hot, garnished with avocado slices and chopped cilantro.

SOPA DE BOLAS DE VERDE

Ingredients

- Green plantains - 3, peeled and grated.
- Ground beef - 1/2 lb.
- Beef broth - 6 cups.
- Carrot - 1/2 cup, diced.
- Bell pepper - 1/2, diced.
- Onion - 1/2 cup, chopped.

- Garlic - 2 cloves, minced.
- Cumin - 1 teaspoon.
- Salt and pepper - to taste.
- Cilantro - 1/4 cup, chopped.
- Egg - 1, for plantain dough.

Instructions

1. Mix grated plantains with the egg, salt, and pepper. Form this mixture into balls, with a portion of the ground beef stuffed in the center of each ball.

2. In a large pot, sauté onions, garlic, carrots, and bell pepper until soft.

3. Add the beef broth and bring to a boil. Gently drop the plantain balls into the broth.

4. Simmer for about 30 minutes, or until the balls are cooked through. Season with cumin, salt, and pepper.

5. Serve hot, sprinkled with chopped cilantro.

CALDO DE PATAS

Ingredients

- Cow's feet - 2, cleaned and cut into pieces.
- Onion - 1, chopped.
- Garlic - 3 cloves, minced.
- Yucca - 1 cup, diced.
- Cilantro - 1/4 cup, chopped.
- Green onion - 1/4 cup, chopped.
- Water - 8 cups.
- Salt and pepper - to taste.
- Oranges - 2, juiced.

Instructions

1. In a large pot, combine the cow's feet with water and bring to a boil. Skim off any foam that forms on the surface.

2. Add the onion, garlic, and simmer until the meat is tender, about 2-3 hours.

3. Add the yucca, and cook until soft.

4. Season with salt, pepper, and orange juice. Stir in cilantro and green onion just before serving.

5. Serve hot.

SOPA DE QUINUA

Ingredients

- Quinoa - 1 cup, rinsed.
- Vegetable broth - 6 cups.
- Carrot - 1/2 cup, diced.
- Potato - 1/2 cup, diced.
- Tomato - 1/2 cup, diced.
- Onion - 1/4 cup, finely chopped.
- Garlic - 2 cloves, minced.
- Cumin - 1 teaspoon.
- Salt and pepper - to taste.
- Avocado - 1, sliced for garnish.
- Cilantro - for garnish.

Instructions

1. In a large pot, sauté onion and garlic until soft.

2. Add the vegetable broth, quinoa, carrots, potatoes, and

tomatoes. Bring to a boil.

3. Reduce heat and simmer until the quinoa and vegetables are cooked, about 20 minutes.

4. Season with cumin, salt, and pepper.

5. Serve hot, garnished with avocado slices and cilantro.

AGUADO DE GALLINA

Ingredients

- Chicken - 2 lbs, cut into pieces.
- Rice - 1 cup.
- Onion - 1, chopped.
- Tomato - 1, chopped.
- Green bell pepper - 1, chopped.
- Garlic - 3 cloves, minced.
- Carrots - 1/2 cup, diced.
- Peas - 1/2 cup.
- Water - 8 cups.
- Salt and pepper - to taste.
- Cilantro - 1/4 cup, chopped for garnish.

Instructions

1. In a large pot, brown the chicken pieces. Remove and set aside.

2. In the same pot, sauté the onion, tomato, bell pepper, and garlic until soft.

3. Return the chicken to the pot, add water, and bring to a boil. Simmer until the chicken is tender, about 30 minutes.

4. Add the rice, carrots, and peas, and cook until the rice is tender, about 20 minutes.

5. Season with salt and pepper.

6. Serve hot, garnished with chopped cilantro.

SOPA DE LENTEJAS

Ingredients

- Lentils - 2 cups, rinsed.
- Water or broth - 6 cups.
- Onion - 1, diced.
- Carrots - 2, diced.
- Tomato - 1, diced.
- Garlic cloves - 2, minced.
- Cumin - 1 teaspoon.
- Salt and pepper - to taste.
- Olive oil - 2 tablespoons.

Instructions

1. Heat the olive oil in a large pot over medium heat. Add the onions, carrots, and garlic, cooking until softened.

2. Add the lentils, water or broth, tomatoes, cumin, salt, and pepper.

3. Bring to a boil, then reduce heat and simmer until lentils are tender, about 30 minutes.

4. Adjust seasoning to taste and serve hot.

CALDO DE BOLAS DE VERDE

Ingredients

- Green plantains - 3, peeled and grated.
- Ground beef - 1/2 lb.
- Beef broth - 8 cups.
- Carrots - 1/2 cup, diced.
- Bell peppers - 1/2 cup, diced.
- Onion - 1, diced.
- Garlic cloves - 2, minced.
- Cilantro - 1/4 cup, chopped.
- Salt and pepper - to taste.
- Egg - 1, beaten (for plantain dough).

Instructions

1. In a bowl, mix grated plantains with the beaten egg, salt, and pepper to form a dough.

2. Take small portions of the dough, flatten them, add a bit of ground beef in the center, and form them into balls.

3. In a large pot, sauté onions, garlic, carrots, and bell peppers until soft.

4. Add beef broth to the sautéed vegetables and bring to a boil.

5. Carefully add the plantain balls to the boiling broth and cook for about 30 minutes, or until they float to the surface.

6. Garnish with cilantro before serving.

SOPA DE FIDEOS

Ingredients

- Angel hair pasta - 1 cup, broken into pieces.
- Chicken broth - 6 cups.
- Carrots - 1/2 cup, diced.
- Potatoes - 1/2 cup, diced.
- Onion - 1/4 cup, finely chopped.
- Tomato sauce - 1/2 cup.
- Olive oil - 2 tablespoons.
- Salt and pepper - to taste.

Instructions

1. In a pot, heat the olive oil over medium heat. Add the broken pasta and toast until golden brown, stirring frequently.

2. Add the onions and carrots, sauté until they are soft.

3. Pour in the chicken broth and bring to a boil. Add the potatoes and tomato sauce.

4. Reduce heat and simmer until the pasta and vegetables are tender, about 15 minutes.

5. Season with salt and pepper to taste. Serve hot.

MENESTRA DE LENTEJAS

Ingredients

- Lentils - 2 cups.
- Water - 4 cups.
- Onion - 1, chopped.
- Garlic cloves - 2, minced.

- Tomato - 1, chopped.
- Red bell pepper - 1, chopped.
- Cumin - 1/2 teaspoon.
- Salt and pepper - to taste.
- Oil - 2 tablespoons.

Instructions

1. Rinse the lentils and drain.

2. In a pot, heat the oil over medium heat. Sauté the onion, garlic, tomato, and red bell pepper until the onion is translucent.

3. Add the lentils, water, cumin, salt, and pepper. Bring to a boil.

4. Reduce the heat and simmer until the lentils are tender, about 25 minutes.

5. Adjust the seasoning and serve warm.

CHUPE DE PESCADO

Ingredients

- Fish fillets - 2 lbs, cut into pieces.
- Onion - 1, chopped.
- Tomato - 1, chopped.
- Garlic cloves - 2, minced.
- Peas - 1/2 cup.
- Carrots - 1/2 cup, diced.
- Rice - 1/2 cup.
- Potatoes - 1 cup, diced.
- Cilantro - 1/4 cup, chopped.
- Water or fish broth - 8 cups.
- Olive oil - 2 tablespoons.

- Salt and pepper - to taste.

Instructions

1. In a large pot, heat the olive oil over medium heat. Sauté the onion, garlic, and tomato until the onion is soft.

2. Add the water or fish broth and bring to a boil. Add the rice, peas, carrots, and potatoes. Simmer until the vegetables are tender, about 20 minutes.

3. Add the fish pieces to the pot and cook until the fish is done, about 10 minutes.

4. Stir in the chopped cilantro, and season with salt and pepper to taste.

5. Serve hot.

SOPA DE GUANDÚ

Ingredients

- Guandú (pigeon peas) - 2 cups, canned or fresh.
- Water or broth - 6 cups.
- Pork ribs - 1 lb, cut into pieces.
- Green plantain - 1, peeled and cut into chunks.
- Yucca - 1 cup, peeled and diced.
- Onion - 1, chopped.
- Garlic cloves - 2, minced.
- Cumin - 1 teaspoon.
- Coriander - 1/4 cup, chopped.
- Salt and pepper - to taste.

Instructions

1. In a large pot, add the pork ribs, onion, garlic, cumin,

salt, pepper, and water or broth. Bring to a boil and then simmer for about 30 minutes.

2. Add the guandú, green plantain, and yucca. Continue to simmer until the vegetables are tender, about 20-30 minutes.

3. Adjust the seasoning if necessary and stir in the chopped coriander before serving.

4. Serve hot.

CREMA DE ACHOJCHA

Ingredients

- Achojcha (Cyclanthera pedata) - 2 cups, sliced.
- Chicken broth - 4 cups.
- Potato - 1, diced.
- Onion - 1, diced.
- Garlic cloves - 2, minced.
- Heavy cream - 1/2 cup.
- Olive oil - 2 tablespoons.
- Salt and pepper - to taste.

Instructions

1. In a pot, heat the olive oil over medium heat and sauté the onion and garlic until they are soft.

2. Add the achojcha and potato, cook for a few minutes.

3. Pour in the chicken broth and bring to a boil. Reduce the heat and simmer until the potato is tender, about 20 minutes.

4. Blend the soup until smooth, return to the pot, and stir

in the heavy cream. Heat through.

5. Season with salt and pepper to taste and serve hot.

SOPA DE ZAPALLO

Ingredients

- Zapallo (squash) - 2 cups, cubed.
- Water or vegetable broth - 4 cups.
- Carrot - 1, diced.
- Onion - 1/2, diced.
- Garlic cloves - 2, minced.
- Cumin - 1/2 teaspoon.
- Heavy cream - 1/4 cup (optional).
- Coriander - 1/4 cup, chopped.
- Salt and pepper - to taste.

Instructions

1. In a large pot, bring the water or vegetable broth to a boil. Add the zapallo, carrot, onion, and garlic. Simmer until the vegetables are tender, about 25 minutes.

2. Blend the soup until smooth, then return it to the pot and bring back to a simmer. If using, stir in the heavy cream.

3. Season with cumin, salt, and pepper to taste.

4. Serve hot, garnished with chopped coriander.

CALDO DE 31

Ingredients

- Beef bones with marrow - 2 lbs.

- Water - 8 cups.
- Yucca - 1 cup, diced.
- Plantains - 2, green, peeled and cut into chunks.
- Peanuts - 1/2 cup, ground.
- Onion - 1, chopped.
- Garlic cloves - 3, minced.
- Cumin - 1 teaspoon.
- Coriander - 1/4 cup, chopped.
- Salt and pepper - to taste.

Instructions

1. In a large pot, add the beef bones, water, onion, garlic, and cumin. Bring to a boil, reduce heat, and simmer for 1 hour.

2. Add the yucca, plantains, and ground peanuts to the pot. Simmer until the vegetables are tender, about 30 minutes.

3. Adjust the seasoning with salt and pepper.

4. Serve hot, garnished with chopped coriander.

SOPA DE POLLO CON NOODLES DE PAPA

Ingredients

- Chicken breast - 1 lb, cut into pieces.
- Water or chicken broth - 6 cups.
- Potato - 2, grated into noodles.
- Carrot - 1, sliced.
- Onion - 1, chopped.
- Garlic cloves - 2, minced.
- Cumin - 1 teaspoon.
- Salt and pepper - to taste.
- Coriander - 1/4 cup, chopped for garnish.

Instructions

1. In a large pot, combine the chicken, water or broth, onion, and garlic. Bring to a boil, then reduce heat and simmer for 20 minutes.

2. Add the grated potato noodles and carrot to the pot. Cook until the potatoes are tender, about 10 minutes.

3. Season with cumin, salt, and pepper.

4. Serve hot, garnished with chopped coriander.

SOPA DE GUANDÚ

Ingredients

- Guandú (pigeon peas) - 2 cups, canned or fresh.
- Water or broth - 6 cups.
- Pork ribs - 1 lb, cut into pieces.
- Green plantain - 1, peeled and cut into chunks.
- Yucca - 1 cup, peeled and diced.
- Onion - 1, chopped.
- Garlic cloves - 2, minced.
- Cumin - 1 teaspoon.
- Coriander - 1/4 cup, chopped.
- Salt and pepper - to taste.

Instructions

1. In a large pot, add the pork ribs, onion, garlic, cumin, salt, pepper, and water or broth. Bring to a boil and then simmer for about 30 minutes.

2. Add the guandú, green plantain, and yucca. Continue to simmer until the vegetables are tender, about 20-30 minutes.

3. Adjust the seasoning if necessary and stir in the chopped coriander before serving.

4. Serve hot.

CREMA DE ACHOJCHA

Ingredients

- Achojcha (Cyclanthera pedata) - 2 cups, sliced.
- Chicken broth - 4 cups.
- Potato - 1, diced.
- Onion - 1, diced.
- Garlic cloves - 2, minced.
- Heavy cream - 1/2 cup.
- Olive oil - 2 tablespoons.
- Salt and pepper - to taste.

Instructions

1. In a pot, heat the olive oil over medium heat and sauté the onion and garlic until they are soft.

2. Add the achojcha and potato, cook for a few minutes.

3. Pour in the chicken broth and bring to a boil. Reduce the heat and simmer until the potato is tender, about 20 minutes.

4. Blend the soup until smooth, return to the pot, and stir in the heavy cream. Heat through.

5. Season with salt and pepper to taste and serve hot.

SOPA DE ZAPALLO

Ingredients

- Zapallo (squash) - 2 cups, cubed.
- Water or vegetable broth - 4 cups.
- Carrot - 1, diced.
- Onion - 1/2, diced.
- Garlic cloves - 2, minced.
- Cumin - 1/2 teaspoon.
- Heavy cream - 1/4 cup (optional).
- Coriander - 1/4 cup, chopped.
- Salt and pepper - to taste.

Instructions

1. In a large pot, bring the water or vegetable broth to a boil. Add the zapallo, carrot, onion, and garlic. Simmer until the vegetables are tender, about 25 minutes.

2. Blend the soup until smooth, then return it to the pot and bring back to a simmer. If using, stir in the heavy cream.

3. Season with cumin, salt, and pepper to taste.

4. Serve hot, garnished with chopped coriander.

CALDO DE 31

Ingredients

- Beef bones with marrow - 2 lbs.
- Water - 8 cups.
- Yucca - 1 cup, diced.
- Plantains - 2, green, peeled and cut into chunks.
- Peanuts - 1/2 cup, ground.

- Onion - 1, chopped.
- Garlic cloves - 3, minced.
- Cumin - 1 teaspoon.
- Coriander - 1/4 cup, chopped.
- Salt and pepper - to taste.

Instructions

1. In a large pot, add the beef bones, water, onion, garlic, and cumin. Bring to a boil, reduce heat, and simmer for 1 hour.

2. Add the yucca, plantains, and ground peanuts to the pot. Simmer until the vegetables are tender, about 30 minutes.

3. Adjust the seasoning with salt and pepper.

4. Serve hot, garnished with chopped coriander.

SOPA DE POLLO CON NOODLES DE PAPA

Ingredients

- Chicken breast - 1 lb, cut into pieces.
- Water or chicken broth - 6 cups.
- Potato - 2, grated into noodles.
- Carrot - 1, sliced.
- Onion - 1, chopped.
- Garlic cloves - 2, minced.
- Cumin - 1 teaspoon.
- Salt and pepper - to taste.
- Coriander - 1/4 cup, chopped for garnish.

Instructions

1. In a large pot, combine the chicken, water or broth,

onion, and garlic. Bring to a boil, then reduce heat and simmer for 20 minutes.

2. Add the grated potato noodles and carrot to the pot. Cook until the potatoes are tender, about 10 minutes.

3. Season with cumin, salt, and pepper.

4. Serve hot, garnished with chopped coriander.

BROTHS

In Ecuadorian cuisine, broths occupy a special place, embodying the essence of simplicity and nourishment. These clear soups are delicately prepared, utilizing a variety of local ingredients that imbue them with a rich, comforting flavor unique to Ecuador's culinary landscape. The preparation of broths involves simmering meats, vegetables, and herbs, allowing the ingredients' natural flavors to meld into a light yet deeply satisfying liquid.

The versatility and nutritional value of Ecuadorian broths are unparalleled, serving as the base for numerous traditional dishes or enjoyed on their own for their restorative properties. They are a testament to the Ecuadorian approach to cooking, where health and flavor coexist harmoniously. Rich in vitamins and minerals, these broths are a testament to the art of maximizing the nutritional benefits of simple ingredients, promoting well-being with every sip.

Ecuadorian broths thus represent a fundamental aspect of healthy eating, demonstrating how culinary traditions can contribute to a balanced diet. Their rich flavors and nutritional benefits affirm the role of broths in Ecuadorian cuisine, not just as a meal component but as a celebration of the country's rich biodiversity and culinary heritage.

CALDO DE PATA

Ingredients

- Cow's feet - 2, cleaned and cut into pieces.
- Water - 8 cups.
- Onion - 1, chopped.

- Garlic cloves - 3, minced.
- Carrots - 2, peeled and chopped.
- Cilantro - 1/4 cup, chopped.
- Parsley - 1/4 cup, chopped.
- Green onions - 2, chopped.
- Yucca - 2 cups, peeled and cut into chunks.
- Salt and pepper - to taste.

Instructions

1. Place the cow's feet in a large pot with the water and bring to a boil. Reduce the heat to a simmer and cook until the meat is tender, about 2 hours.

2. Add the onion, garlic, carrots, yucca, salt, and pepper. Continue to simmer until the vegetables are tender, about 30 minutes.

3. Add the cilantro, parsley, and green onions. Simmer for an additional 10 minutes.

4. Adjust seasoning to taste and serve hot.

CALDO DE MANGUERA

Ingredients

- Pork intestines - 2 lbs, cleaned thoroughly.
- Water - 6 cups.
- Onion - 1, chopped.
- Garlic cloves - 4, minced.
- Coriander - 1/4 cup, chopped.
- Cumin - 1 teaspoon.
- Pepper - 1 teaspoon.
- Salt - to taste.

Instructions

1. In a large pot, boil the pork intestines in water for about 10 minutes. Drain and rinse.

2. Return the intestines to the pot, add fresh water, onion, garlic, cumin, pepper, and salt. Bring to a boil, then reduce to a simmer and cook until the intestines are tender, about 1.5 hours.

3. Add the chopped coriander a few minutes before finishing the cooking.

4. Adjust seasoning to taste and serve hot.

CALDO DE GALLINA CRIOLLA

Ingredients

- Free-range chicken - 1, cut into pieces.
- Water - 8 cups.
- Onion - 1, quartered.
- Garlic cloves - 3, crushed.
- Carrots - 2, chopped.
- Green peas - 1/2 cup.
- Potatoes - 3, peeled and quartered.
- Salt and pepper - to taste.
- Cilantro - 1/4 cup, chopped for garnish.

Instructions

1. In a large pot, combine the chicken pieces, water, onion, and garlic. Bring to a boil, then reduce the heat and simmer until the chicken is almost tender, about 40 minutes.

2. Add the carrots, green peas, and potatoes to the pot.

Continue to simmer until the vegetables are tender, about 20 minutes.

3. Season with salt and pepper to taste.

4. Garnish with chopped cilantro and serve hot.

YAGUARLOCRO

Ingredients

- Lamb tripe - 2 lbs, cleaned and chopped.
- Water - 6 cups.
- Onion - 1, chopped.
- Peanut butter - 1/4 cup.
- Potatoes - 4, peeled and diced.
- Garlic cloves - 3, minced.
- Cumin - 1 teaspoon.
- Achiote (annatto) - 1 teaspoon.
- Salt and pepper - to taste.
- Avocado and cilantro for garnish.

Instructions

1. In a large pot, boil the lamb tripe in water until tender, about 2 hours.

2. Add the onion, garlic, cumin, achiote, salt, and pepper. Simmer for an additional 30 minutes.

3. Add the peanut butter and potatoes, cook until the potatoes are tender, about 20 minutes.

4. Adjust seasoning to taste. Serve hot, garnished with avocado slices and cilantro.

CALDO DE BAGRE

Ingredients

- Catfish - 2 lbs, cleaned and cut into pieces.
- Water - 8 cups.
- Onion - 1, chopped.
- Tomatoes - 2, chopped.
- Green bell pepper - 1, chopped.
- Garlic cloves - 3, minced.
- Coriander - 1/4 cup, chopped.
- Cumin - 1 teaspoon.
- Salt and pepper - to taste.

Instructions

1. In a large pot, combine the water, catfish, onion, tomatoes, green bell pepper, and garlic. Bring to a boil, then reduce the heat and simmer until the fish is cooked through, about 30 minutes.

2. Season with cumin, salt, and pepper. Add the chopped coriander a few minutes before the soup is done.

3. Adjust seasoning to taste and serve hot.

CALDO DE SALCHICHA

Ingredients

- Beef sausages - 4, sliced.
- Potatoes - 2, diced.
- Carrots - 2, sliced.
- Onion - 1, diced.
- Garlic cloves - 2, minced.
- Water - 6 cups.
- Cumin - 1 teaspoon.

- Salt and pepper - to taste.
- Cilantro - 1/4 cup, chopped for garnish.

Instructions

1. In a large pot, bring water to a boil. Add the sausages, potatoes, carrots, onion, and garlic.

2. Season with cumin, salt, and pepper. Simmer for about 30 minutes or until the vegetables are tender.

3. Adjust the seasoning to taste. Serve hot, garnished with chopped cilantro.

AGUADO DE GALLINA

Ingredients

- Hen - 1, cut into pieces.
- Rice - 1 cup.
- Carrots - 2, sliced.
- Peas - 1/2 cup.
- Potatoes - 3, diced.
- Onion - 1, chopped.
- Garlic cloves - 3, minced.
- Water - 8 cups.
- Salt and pepper - to taste.
- Cilantro - 1/4 cup, chopped for garnish.

Instructions

1. In a large pot, place the hen pieces and water. Bring to a boil, then simmer for about 1 hour or until the chicken is tender.

2. Add the rice, carrots, peas, potatoes, onion, and garlic to the pot. Season with salt and pepper.

3. Continue to simmer until the rice and vegetables are cooked, about 30 minutes.

4. Adjust the seasoning to taste. Serve hot, garnished with chopped cilantro.

CALDO DE GUAGUAS

Ingredients

- Corn dough - 2 cups.
- Chicken broth - 6 cups.
- Onion - 1, finely chopped.
- Garlic cloves - 2, minced.
- Pork lard - 1 tablespoon.
- Salt - 1 teaspoon.
- Cumin - 1/2 teaspoon.

Instructions

1. In a large pot, heat the pork lard over medium heat. Add the onion and garlic, sautéing until translucent.

2. Pour in the chicken broth and bring to a boil. Gradually add the corn dough, stirring continuously to avoid lumps.

3. Season with salt and cumin. Reduce the heat and simmer for about 20 minutes, or until the soup thickens.

4. Serve hot.

CALDO DE CUERO

Ingredients

- Cow hides - 2 lbs, cleaned and cut into pieces.

- Water - 8 cups.
- Onion - 1, chopped.
- Tomatoes - 2, chopped.
- Garlic cloves - 3, minced.
- Peanuts - 1/2 cup, ground.
- Cumin - 1 teaspoon.
- Salt and pepper - to taste.

Instructions

1. In a large pot, cover the cow hides with water and bring to a boil. Reduce heat and simmer until the hides are tender, about 2 hours.

2. Add the onion, tomatoes, garlic, ground peanuts, cumin, salt, and pepper. Continue to simmer for another 30 minutes.

3. Adjust the seasoning to taste. Serve hot.

CONSOMÉ DE POLLO

Ingredients

- Chicken bones - 2 lbs.
- Water - 10 cups.
- Carrots - 2, chopped.
- Onion - 1, quartered.
- Celery stalks - 2, chopped.
- Garlic cloves - 2, crushed.
- Bay leaves - 2.
- Salt - 1 teaspoon.
- Peppercorns - 1 teaspoon.

Instructions

1. In a large pot, combine the chicken bones, water,

carrots, onion, celery, garlic, bay leaves, salt, and peppercorns. Bring to a boil.

2. Reduce heat and simmer for at least 2 hours, skimming off any foam that forms on the surface.

3. Strain the broth through a fine sieve to remove the solids. Adjust the seasoning to taste.

4. Serve hot or use as a base for other dishes.

CALDO DE PEZ VELA

Ingredients

- Sailfish - 2 lbs, cut into pieces.
- Water - 8 cups.
- Onions - 2, chopped.
- Tomatoes - 3, chopped.
- Green peppers - 2, chopped.
- Garlic cloves - 4, minced.
- Cilantro - 1/4 cup, chopped.
- Salt and pepper - to taste.
- Lime - 2, juiced.

Instructions

1. In a large pot, bring the water to a boil. Add the sailfish pieces, onions, tomatoes, green peppers, and garlic.

2. Lower the heat and simmer until the fish is cooked through, about 30 minutes.

3. Season with salt and pepper. Add the lime juice and cilantro before serving.

4. Serve hot.

CALDO DE COSTILLA

Ingredients

- Beef ribs - 3 lbs.
- Water - 10 cups.
- Potatoes - 4, cubed.
- Carrots - 2, sliced.
- Onion - 1, chopped.
- Garlic cloves - 3, minced.
- Cilantro - 1/4 cup, chopped.
- Salt and pepper - to taste.

Instructions

1. In a large pot, place the beef ribs and water. Bring to a boil, then reduce heat to simmer.

2. After 1 hour of cooking, add the potatoes, carrots, onion, and garlic. Continue to simmer until the vegetables are tender, about 30 minutes.

3. Season with salt and pepper to taste. Add the cilantro just before serving.

4. Serve the broth hot.

CALDO TLALPEÑO ECUATORIANO

Ingredients

- Chicken breast - 2, shredded.
- Chicken broth - 8 cups.
- Carrots - 2, diced.
- Zucchini - 2, diced.
- Chipotle peppers in adobo sauce - 2, chopped.
- White rice - 1/2 cup.

- Avocado - 1, sliced.
- Queso fresco - 1/2 cup, crumbled.
- Lime - 2, cut into wedges.
- Cilantro - 1/4 cup, chopped.
- Salt - to taste.

Instructions

1. In a large pot, bring the chicken broth to a boil. Add the shredded chicken, carrots, zucchini, and chipotle peppers. Simmer for about 20 minutes.

2. Add the rice and continue to cook until the rice is tender, about 15 minutes.

3. Season with salt. Serve the broth in bowls, garnished with avocado slices, crumbled queso fresco, lime wedges, and cilantro.

4. Serve hot.

CALDO DE HUESO DE RES

Ingredients

- Beef bones with marrow - 4 lbs.
- Water - 12 cups.
- Onion - 1, quartered.
- Carrots - 3, chopped.
- Celery - 2 stalks, chopped.
- Garlic - 4 cloves, crushed.
- Bouquet garni (thyme, bay leaf, parsley) - 1.
- Salt and pepper - to taste.

Instructions

1. In a large pot, place the beef bones and cover with

water. Bring to a boil, then reduce to a simmer.

2. Add the onion, carrots, celery, garlic, and bouquet garni. Simmer for 3-4 hours, skimming the surface as necessary.

3. Strain the broth and season with salt and pepper to taste.

4. Serve hot, optionally with bread on the side.

CALDO DE CAMARÓN

Ingredients

- Shrimp - 2 lbs, peeled and deveined.
- Water - 8 cups.
- Onion - 1, chopped.
- Tomato - 2, chopped.
- Bell pepper - 1, chopped.
- Carrots - 2, sliced.
- Garlic cloves - 3, minced.
- Cilantro - 1/4 cup, chopped.
- Salt and pepper - to taste.
- Lime - 2, juiced.

Instructions

1. In a large pot, bring water to a boil. Add the onion, tomato, bell pepper, carrots, and garlic. Simmer for 20 minutes.

2. Add the shrimp and cook until they are pink and cooked through, about 5 minutes.

3. Season with salt and pepper. Add the lime juice and cilantro just before serving. 4. Serve hot.

SEAFOOD DISHES

Ecuadorian seafood dishes stand as a testament to the country's rich maritime heritage, showcasing an exceptional variety of fish and shellfish from its extensive coastline. These dishes are celebrated for their fresh flavors and the skillful way they are combined with local produce and spices, creating a distinctive taste profile that sets them apart. The meticulous preparation of each seafood dish, whether it's ceviche, a marinated seafood delight, or a hearty fish stew, reflects Ecuador's respect for the ocean's bounty and its pivotal role in the culinary landscape.

The versatility of Ecuadorian seafood is remarkable, with each dish offering a unique exploration of textures and flavors that cater to a wide array of palates. This diversity not only highlights the abundance of seafood available but also underscores the adaptability of Ecuadorian cuisine to incorporate healthful, nutrient-rich ingredients. Seafood dishes in Ecuador are a source of essential proteins, omega-3 fatty acids, and other vital nutrients, contributing to a balanced and nutritious diet.

Therefore, Ecuadorian seafood dishes are more than just meals; they are a celebration of the country's coastal resources and culinary creativity. Their rich nutritional profile and exceptional flavors exemplify the harmonious blend of tradition and nourishment found in Ecuadorian cooking.

CEVICHE DE CAMARÓN

Ingredients

- Shrimp - 2 lbs, cooked and peeled.

- Lime juice - 1 cup.
- Tomato - 2, diced.
- Red onion - 1, thinly sliced.
- Cilantro - 1/4 cup, chopped.
- Orange juice - 1/2 cup.
- Salt and pepper - to taste.
- Ketchup - 2 tablespoons (optional).

Instructions

1. In a large bowl, mix the cooked shrimp with lime juice and orange juice. Let it marinate for about 10 minutes.

2. Add the diced tomato, sliced red onion, chopped cilantro, and ketchup if using. Mix well.

3. Season with salt and pepper to taste.

4. Refrigerate for at least one hour before serving. Serve cold.

ENCOCADO DE PESCADO

Ingredients

- Fish fillets - 2 lbs.
- Coconut milk - 2 cups.
- Onion - 1, sliced.
- Tomato - 2, diced.
- Bell pepper - 1, sliced.
- Garlic cloves - 3, minced.
- Cumin - 1 teaspoon.
- Coriander - 1/4 cup, chopped.
- Salt and pepper - to taste.

Instructions

1. Season the fish fillets with salt and pepper.

2. In a large skillet, sauté the onion, bell pepper, and garlic until soft.

3. Add the diced tomato and cumin, cook for a few minutes.

4. Pour in the coconut milk and bring to a simmer.

5. Add the fish fillets to the skillet, cover, and simmer until the fish is cooked through, about 15 minutes.

6. Garnish with chopped coriander before serving. Serve hot.

CEVICHE DE PESCADO

Ingredients

- Fish fillets - 2 lbs, cut into small pieces.
- Lime juice - 1 cup.
- Tomato - 3, diced.
- Red onion - 1, thinly sliced.
- Cilantro - 1/4 cup, chopped.
- Orange juice - 1/2 cup.
- Salt and pepper - to taste.
- Hot pepper - 1, sliced (optional).

Instructions

1. In a large bowl, combine the fish pieces with lime juice and orange juice. Allow to marinate for about 20 minutes in the refrigerator.

2. Add the diced tomato, sliced red onion, chopped cilantro, and hot pepper if using. Mix well.

3. Season with salt and pepper to taste.

4. Refrigerate for an additional hour before serving. Serve cold.

CORVICHE

Ingredients

- Green plantains - 5, peeled and grated.
- Fish - 1 lb, cooked and shredded.
- Onion - 1, finely chopped.
- Garlic cloves - 2, minced.
- Cumin - 1 teaspoon.
- Coriander - 1/4 cup, chopped.
- Salt and pepper - to taste.
- Oil - for frying.

Instructions

1. Mix the grated plantains with salt. Form into balls, then flatten them to create discs.

2. Mix the cooked, shredded fish with onion, garlic, cumin, coriander, salt, and pepper.

3. Place a spoonful of the fish mixture on each plantain disc, fold it over, and seal the edges to form a corviche.

4. Heat oil in a deep fryer or large skillet. Fry the corviches until they are golden brown on all sides.

5. Drain on paper towels and serve hot.

ENCEBOLLADO

Ingredients

- Fresh tuna - 2 lbs, cut into chunks.
- Water - 8 cups.
- Cassava (yucca) - 2 lbs, peeled and chopped.
- Red onions - 2, thinly sliced.
- Tomatoes - 2, chopped.
- Coriander - 1/2 cup, chopped.
- Lime juice - 1/2 cup.
- Salt and pepper - to taste.
- Oil - 2 tablespoons.

Instructions

1. In a large pot, cook the tuna chunks in water until they are just done, about 20 minutes. Remove the tuna and set aside.

2. In the same water, cook the cassava until tender, about 30 minutes. Remove and set aside.

3. In a separate pan, sauté the onions and tomatoes in oil until soft.

4. Return the tuna and cassava to the pot. Add the sautéed onions, tomatoes, coriander, lime juice, salt, and pepper. Simmer for about 10 minutes to blend the flavors.

5. Serve hot.

CEVICHE DE CONCHA

Ingredients

- Black clams (conchas) - 2 lbs, cleaned.

- Lime juice - 1 cup.
- Orange juice - 1/2 cup.
- Onion - 1, finely chopped.
- Tomatoes - 2, diced.
- Green pepper - 1, diced.
- Cilantro - 1/4 cup, chopped.
- Salt and pepper - to taste.

Instructions

1. Rinse the black clams thoroughly in cold water.

2. Mix the clams with lime juice and orange juice. Let marinate for 30 minutes in the refrigerator.

3. Add the onion, tomatoes, green pepper, and cilantro. Season with salt and pepper.

4. Mix well and let it sit for an additional 10 minutes before serving.

5. Serve cold, garnished with extra cilantro if desired.

CAZUELA DE MARISCOS

Ingredients

- Mixed seafood (shrimp, squid, clams) - 2 lbs.
- Coconut milk - 2 cups.
- Onion - 1, diced.
- Garlic cloves - 3, minced.
- Red pepper - 1, diced.
- Tomatoes - 2, diced.
- Annatto (achiote) oil - 2 tablespoons.
- Cumin - 1 teaspoon.
- Cilantro - 1/4 cup, chopped.
- Salt and pepper - to taste.

Instructions

1. In a large pot, heat the annatto oil over medium heat. Sauté the onion, garlic, and red pepper until soft.

2. Add the tomatoes and cook until they break down, about 5 minutes.

3. Pour in the coconut milk and bring to a simmer. Add the seafood, cover, and cook until just done, about 10 minutes.

4. Season with cumin, salt, and pepper. Stir in the cilantro just before serving.

5. Serve hot, accompanied by rice or plantain slices.

CEVICHE DE LANGOSTINOS

Ingredients

- Prawns - 2 lbs, peeled and deveined.
- Lime juice - 1 cup.
- Orange juice - 1/2 cup.
- Red onion - 1, thinly sliced.
- Tomatoes - 2, diced.
- Cucumber - 1, diced.
- Jalapeño - 1, minced (optional).
- Cilantro - 1/4 cup, chopped.
- Salt and pepper - to taste.

Instructions

1. Blanch the prawns in boiling water for 2 minutes, then transfer to ice water to stop the cooking process.

2. Combine the prawns with lime juice and orange juice

in a bowl. Refrigerate for 30 minutes to marinate.

3. Add the red onion, tomatoes, cucumber, jalapeño (if using), and cilantro to the prawns. Season with salt and pepper.

4. Mix well and let it sit for an additional 10 minutes in the fridge before serving.

5. Serve cold, garnished with slices of avocado if desired.

PESCADO ENCOCADO

Ingredients

- Fish fillets - 2 lbs.
- Coconut milk - 2 cups.
- Onion - 1, sliced.
- Bell pepper - 1, sliced.
- Garlic cloves - 3, minced.
- Tomato - 1, chopped.
- Cumin - 1/2 teaspoon.
- Cilantro - 1/4 cup, chopped.
- Lime - 1, juiced.
- Salt and pepper - to taste.

Instructions

1. Season the fish fillets with salt, pepper, and lime juice.

2. In a large skillet, sauté the onion, bell pepper, and garlic until soft.

3. Add the tomato and cook for another 2 minutes.

4. Pour in the coconut milk and bring to a simmer. Add the fish fillets to the skillet, cover, and simmer until the

fish is cooked through, about 15 minutes.

5. Garnish with cilantro before serving.

6. Serve hot with rice or plantains.

SUDADO DE PESCADO

Ingredients

- Fish fillets - 2 lbs.
- Onion - 2, sliced.
- Tomato - 3, sliced.
- Garlic cloves - 3, minced.
- Yellow pepper paste - 2 tablespoons.
- Beer - 1 cup.
- Cilantro - 1/4 cup, chopped.
- Salt and pepper - to taste.
- Oil - 2 tablespoons.

Instructions

1. Season the fish fillets with salt and pepper.

2. In a large skillet, heat the oil over medium heat. Sauté the onion, tomato, and garlic until soft.

3. Add the yellow pepper paste and cook for 1 minute.

4. Place the fish fillets on top of the vegetable mixture. Pour the beer over the fish.

5. Cover and simmer for about 20 minutes or until the fish is cooked through.

6. Garnish with cilantro and serve hot, accompanied by white rice or boiled potatoes.

CEVICHE DE CALAMAR

Ingredients

- Squid - 2 lbs, cleaned and sliced into rings.
- Lime juice - 1 cup.
- Orange juice - 1/2 cup.
- Red onion - 1, thinly sliced.
- Tomatoes - 2, diced.
- Green chili - 1, minced (optional).
- Cilantro - 1/4 cup, chopped.
- Salt and pepper - to taste.

Instructions

1. Blanch the squid rings in boiling water for 1-2 minutes, then transfer to ice water to stop the cooking process.

2. Combine the squid with lime juice and orange juice in a bowl. Allow to marinate for 20 minutes in the refrigerator.

3. Add the sliced red onion, diced tomatoes, minced green chili (if using), and chopped cilantro. Season with salt and pepper.

4. Mix well and let it sit for an additional 10 minutes in the fridge before serving.

5. Serve cold, garnished with extra cilantro if desired.

CEVICHE DE PULPO

Ingredients

- Octopus - 2 lbs, cooked and sliced.

- Lime juice - 1 cup.
- Orange juice - 1/2 cup.
- Red onion - 1, thinly sliced.
- Cucumber - 1, diced.
- Tomatoes - 2, diced.
- Cilantro - 1/4 cup, chopped.
- Salt and pepper - to taste.

Instructions

1. In a large bowl, combine the cooked octopus with lime juice and orange juice. Allow to marinate for 30 minutes in the refrigerator.

2. Add the sliced red onion, diced cucumber, diced tomatoes, and chopped cilantro. Season with salt and pepper.

3. Mix well and refrigerate for an additional 10 minutes before serving.

4. Serve cold, garnished with slices of avocado or additional cilantro, if desired.

ARROZ MARINERO

Ingredients

- Seafood mix (shrimp, squid, clams) - 2 lbs.
- Rice - 2 cups.
- Chicken broth - 4 cups.
- Onion - 1, diced.
- Garlic cloves - 3, minced.
- Bell pepper - 1, diced.
- Tomato sauce - 1 cup.
- Peas - 1/2 cup.
- Carrots - 1/2 cup, diced.

- Cilantro - 1/4 cup, chopped.
- Salt and pepper - to taste.
- Oil - 2 tablespoons.

Instructions

1. In a large pot, heat the oil over medium heat. Sauté the onion, garlic, and bell pepper until soft.

2. Add the rice and cook, stirring frequently, until it is lightly toasted.

3. Stir in the tomato sauce, chicken broth, peas, and carrots. Bring to a boil.

4. Reduce the heat, cover, and simmer for 20 minutes.

5. Add the seafood mix, cover, and cook for an additional 10 minutes, or until the seafood is cooked through and the rice is tender.

6. Garnish with chopped cilantro before serving. Season with salt and pepper to taste.

7. Serve hot.

SOPA MARINERA

Ingredients

- Mixed seafood (fish, shrimp, squid) - 2 lbs.
- Water - 6 cups.
- Onion - 1, chopped.
- Garlic cloves - 2, minced.
- Tomatoes - 2, diced.
- Bell pepper - 1, diced.
- Potatoes - 2, diced.

- Carrots - 1, diced.
- Cilantro - 1/4 cup, chopped.
- Salt and pepper - to taste.
- Oil - 1 tablespoon.

Instructions

1. In a large pot, heat the oil over medium heat. Add the onion, garlic, tomatoes, and bell pepper. Sauté until soft.

2. Add the water, potatoes, and carrots. Bring to a boil, then reduce the heat and simmer until the vegetables are tender, about 15 minutes.

3. Add the mixed seafood and cook for an additional 10 minutes, or until the seafood is cooked through.

4. Season with salt and pepper. Stir in the chopped cilantro just before serving.

5. Serve hot, accompanied by steamed rice or bread.

CAMARONES AL AJILLO

Ingredients

- Shrimp - 2 lbs, peeled and deveined.
- Garlic - 6 cloves, minced.
- Olive oil - 1/4 cup.
- Butter - 2 tablespoons.
- Red pepper flakes - 1/2 teaspoon (optional).
- Lime - 1, juiced.
- Salt and pepper - to taste.
- Parsley - 1/4 cup, chopped for garnish.

Instructions

1. In a large skillet, heat the olive oil and butter over medium heat. Add the garlic and red pepper flakes, cook until fragrant, about 1 minute.

2. Increase the heat to high, add the shrimp, and sauté until they turn pink and are cooked through, about 3-5 minutes.

3. Season with salt, pepper, and lime juice.

4. Garnish with chopped parsley before serving.

5. Serve hot, accompanied by slices of crusty bread or over cooked rice.

BEEF DISHES

Ecuadorian beef dishes are a celebration of the country's rich pastoral lands and the skillful culinary techniques that have been passed down through generations. These dishes are characterized by their robust flavors and tender textures, achieved through slow-cooking methods that allow the meat's natural qualities to shine. The incorporation of local spices and ingredients, such as achiote and yuca, lends these beef dishes a unique flavor profile that distinguishes them from other global cuisines.

The versatility of beef in Ecuadorian cuisine is evident in the wide array of dishes it stars in, from savory stews to grilled specialties, each highlighting the meat's adaptability and rich nutritional value. This versatility ensures that beef can be enjoyed in numerous forms, catering to different tastes while providing essential nutrients like protein, iron, and B vitamins. Such dishes reflect the balance between indulgence and nutrition, embodying the essence of Ecuadorian culinary tradition.

Accordingly, Ecuadorian beef dishes not only offer a feast for the senses but also play a significant role in a balanced diet. They underscore the culinary richness of Ecuador, showcasing how traditional practices can produce dishes that are both flavorful and nourishing.

LOMO SALTADO

Ingredients

- Beef tenderloin - 2 lbs, sliced into strips.
- Red onion - 1, sliced.
- Tomatoes - 2, sliced.

- Green chili - 1, sliced.
- Garlic cloves - 3, minced.
- Soy sauce - 1/4 cup.
- Vinegar - 2 tablespoons.
- Cilantro - 1/4 cup, chopped.
- Vegetable oil - 2 tablespoons.
- Salt and pepper - to taste.
- Potatoes - 3, cut into fries and fried.

Instructions

1. Heat oil in a large skillet over high heat. Add the beef strips and fry until browned. Remove and set aside.

2. In the same skillet, add the red onion, tomatoes, green chili, and garlic. Cook until the onions are soft.

3. Return the beef to the skillet. Add the soy sauce, vinegar, and season with salt and pepper. Cook for an additional 2-3 minutes.

4. Stir in the cilantro and remove from heat.

5. Serve the lomo saltado over the fried potatoes.

SECO DE CARNE

Ingredients

- Beef chuck - 2 lbs, cut into cubes.
- Beer - 1 cup.
- Orange juice - 1/2 cup.
- Onion - 1, chopped.
- Tomato paste - 2 tablespoons.
- Garlic cloves - 4, minced.
- Coriander - 1/2 cup, chopped.
- Cumin - 1 teaspoon.

- Salt and pepper - to taste.
- Vegetable oil - 2 tablespoons.

Instructions

1. In a pot, heat the oil over medium heat. Add the beef and brown on all sides. Remove and set aside.

2. In the same pot, add the onion and garlic, cooking until soft. Stir in the tomato paste, coriander, cumin, salt, and pepper.

3. Return the beef to the pot. Add the beer and orange juice. Bring to a boil, then reduce to a simmer, cover, and cook until the beef is tender, about 1-2 hours.

4. Serve the seco de carne with rice and avocado slices.

FRITADA

Ingredients

- Pork - 2 lbs, cut into chunks.
- Orange juice - 1 cup.
- Beer - 1/2 cup.
- Garlic cloves - 5, minced.
- Cumin - 1 teaspoon.
- Salt - 1 tablespoon.
- Water - 2 cups.

Instructions

1. In a large pot, combine the pork, orange juice, beer, garlic, cumin, and salt. Add water to cover the pork.

2. Bring to a boil, then reduce the heat to medium-low, cover, and simmer until the pork is tender, about 1 hour.

3. Increase the heat to medium-high and cook until the liquid evaporates and the pork starts to fry in its own fat, turning occasionally until browned.

4. Serve the fritada with boiled potatoes and corn.

CARNE COLORADA

Ingredients

- Beef - 2 lbs, thinly sliced.
- Annatto oil - 1/4 cup.
- Garlic cloves - 3, minced.
- Scallions - 1/2 cup, chopped.
- Beer - 1/2 cup.
- Cumin - 1 teaspoon.
- Salt and pepper - to taste.

Instructions

1. In a bowl, marinate the beef with garlic, scallions, cumin, salt, and pepper. Let it sit for at least 30 minutes.

2. Heat the annatto oil in a skillet over medium-high heat. Add the beef slices and fry until browned on both sides.

3. Pour in the beer, reduce the heat to low, cover, and simmer until the beef is tender, about 30 minutes.

4. Serve the carne colorada with rice and fried plantains.

ESTOFADO DE CARNE

Ingredients

- Beef stew meat - 2 lbs.
- Onion - 1, chopped.

- Carrots - 2, chopped.
- Potatoes - 3, cubed.
- Tomato sauce - 1 cup.
- Beef broth - 2 cups.
- Red wine - 1/2 cup.
- Garlic cloves - 3, minced.
- Bay leaves - 2.
- Thyme - 1 teaspoon.
- Salt and pepper - to taste.
- Olive oil - 2 tablespoons.

Instructions

1. Heat the olive oil in a large pot over medium heat. Add the beef and brown on all sides. Remove and set aside.

2. In the same pot, add the onion, carrots, and garlic. Cook until softened.

3. Return the beef to the pot. Add the tomato sauce, beef broth, red wine, bay leaves, and thyme. Season with salt and pepper.

4. Bring to a boil, then reduce the heat to low, cover, and simmer for 1.5 hours.

5. Add the potatoes and continue to cook until the potatoes are tender, about 30 minutes more.

6. Adjust seasoning and serve hot.

HORNADO

Ingredients

- Pork leg - 5 lbs.
- Garlic cloves - 5, minced.

- Ground cumin - 1 tablespoon.
- Beer - 2 cups.
- Orange juice - 1 cup.
- Salt - 2 tablespoons.
- Pepper - 1 teaspoon.

Instructions

1. Mix garlic, cumin, beer, orange juice, salt, and pepper in a bowl to create a marinade.

2. Rub the marinade all over the pork leg and let it marinate overnight in the refrigerator.

3. Preheat the oven to 350°F (175°C). Place the pork in a roasting pan and cover with aluminum foil.

4. Roast in the preheated oven for about 4 hours, or until the meat is tender and falls off the bone. Remove the foil for the last 30 minutes to brown the outside of the pork.

5. Serve hot, accompanied by potatoes and aji sauce.

GUATITA

Ingredients

- Tripe - 2 lbs, cleaned and cut into pieces.
- Peanut butter - 1/4 cup.
- Potatoes - 3, peeled and diced.
- Onion - 1, finely chopped.
- Tomato paste - 2 tablespoons.
- Cumin - 1 teaspoon.
- Coriander - 1/4 cup, chopped.
- Salt and pepper - to taste.
- Water - 4 cups.

Instructions

1. Boil the tripe in water until tender, about 2 hours. Drain and set aside.

2. In a pot, sauté onions until translucent. Add the tomato paste, cumin, salt, and pepper.

3. Add the cooked tripe and potatoes to the pot. Cover with water and bring to a boil.

4. Reduce the heat and simmer until the potatoes are tender.

5. Stir in the peanut butter and cook for an additional 5 minutes.

6. Garnish with chopped coriander before serving.

ASADO DE RES

Ingredients

- Beef roast - 3 lbs.
- Beer - 1 cup.
- Beef broth - 1 cup.
- Worcestershire sauce - 2 tablespoons.
- Garlic cloves - 4, minced.
- Bay leaves - 2.
- Salt and pepper - to taste.
- Olive oil - 2 tablespoons.

Instructions

1. Season the beef roast with salt and pepper.

2. In a large pan, heat olive oil over medium-high heat.

Brown the roast on all sides.

3. Transfer the roast to a baking dish. Add beer, beef broth, Worcestershire sauce, garlic, and bay leaves around the roast.

4. Cover with aluminum foil and bake in a preheated oven at 350°F (175°C) for about 2 hours, or until the meat is tender.

5. Let it rest before slicing. Serve with the juices from the pan.

BISTEC DE PALOMILLA

Ingredients

- Thin beef steaks - 2 lbs.
- Lime juice - 1/4 cup.
- Garlic cloves - 3, minced.
- Olive oil - 2 tablespoons.
- Salt and pepper - to taste.
- Onions - 2, sliced.

Instructions

1. Marinate the beef steaks with lime juice, garlic, salt, and pepper for at least 30 minutes.

2. Heat olive oil in a skillet over medium-high heat. Cook the steaks for about 2-3 minutes on each side or until they reach the desired doneness.

3. In the same skillet, add a little more oil if needed and sauté the onions until they are soft and golden.

4. Serve the steaks topped with the sautéed onions.

CARNE EN PALITO

Ingredients

- Beef cut into 1-inch cubes - 2 lbs.
- Soy sauce - 1/2 cup.
- Orange juice - 1/4 cup.
- Garlic cloves - 4, minced.
- Cumin - 1 teaspoon.
- Salt and pepper - to taste.
- Wooden skewers - soaked in water for 30 minutes.

Instructions

1. In a bowl, mix soy sauce, orange juice, garlic, cumin, salt, and pepper to create the marinade.

2. Add the beef cubes to the marinade and let them marinate for at least 2 hours in the refrigerator.

3. Thread the marinated beef cubes onto the soaked skewers.

4. Grill the skewers over medium-high heat, turning occasionally, until the beef is cooked to your liking, about 10-15 minutes. 5. Serve hot.

LENGUA EN SALSA DE MANÍ

Ingredients

- Beef tongue - 1 (about 3 lbs).
- Peanut butter - 1/2 cup.
- Onion - 1, finely chopped.
- Tomato - 2, diced.
- Garlic cloves - 3, minced.
- Cumin - 1 teaspoon.

- Coriander - 1/4 cup, chopped.
- Beef broth - 4 cups.
- Salt and pepper - to taste.
- Oil - 2 tablespoons.

Instructions

1. Boil the beef tongue in water until tender, about 2-3 hours. Remove the skin and slice.

2. In a pan, heat the oil and sauté the onion, garlic, tomato, cumin, and coriander until the onion is soft.

3. Add the beef broth and peanut butter to the pan, stirring until the sauce is smooth.

4. Add the sliced tongue to the sauce and simmer for an additional 20 minutes.

5. Season with salt and pepper. Serve hot, garnished with more chopped coriander.

COSTILLAS BBQ ESTILO ECUATORIANO

Ingredients

- Pork ribs - 2 lbs.
- Garlic cloves - 4, minced.
- Orange juice - 1 cup.
- Soy sauce - 1/2 cup.
- Honey - 1/4 cup.
- Smoked paprika - 1 tablespoon.
- Salt and pepper - to taste.

Instructions

1. In a bowl, mix the orange juice, soy sauce, honey,

garlic, smoked paprika, salt, and pepper to create the marinade.

2. Marinate the ribs in the mixture for at least 4 hours, preferably overnight, in the refrigerator.

3. Preheat the oven to 350°F (175°C). Place the ribs on a baking sheet and cover with aluminum foil.

4. Bake for about 1.5 hours or until tender. Remove the foil and increase the oven temperature to broil. Broil for 5-10 minutes to crisp the outside.

5. Serve hot, brushed with extra marinade as sauce.

ROLLO DE CARNE RELLENO

Ingredients

- Ground beef - 2 lbs.
- Bacon - 8 slices.
- Hard-boiled eggs - 4, sliced.
- Carrots - 2, blanched and sliced.
- Spinach - 1 cup, blanched.
- Breadcrumbs - 1/2 cup.
- Garlic cloves - 3, minced.
- Salt and pepper - to taste.
- Eggs - 2, beaten.

Instructions

1. Preheat the oven to 375°F (190°C).

2. In a bowl, mix the ground beef, garlic, breadcrumbs, beaten eggs, salt, and pepper.

3. Flatten the meat mixture on a sheet of plastic wrap to

form a rectangle.

4. Layer the bacon, hard-boiled eggs, carrots, and spinach over the meat.

5. Using the plastic wrap as a guide, roll the meat tightly around the fillings.

6. Place the meat roll in a baking dish and remove the plastic wrap.

7. Bake for about 1 hour or until the meat is cooked through.

8. Let it rest for 10 minutes before slicing. Serve hot.

CHURRASCO ECUATORIANO

Ingredients

- Thinly sliced beef steaks - 2 lbs.
- Garlic cloves - 4, minced.
- Soy sauce - 1/4 cup.
- Worcestershire sauce - 2 tablespoons.
- Orange juice - 1/2 cup.
- Salt and pepper - to taste.
- Olive oil - for frying.

Instructions

1. Marinate the beef steaks in a mixture of garlic, soy sauce, Worcestershire sauce, orange juice, salt, and pepper for at least 1 hour.

2. Heat olive oil in a skillet over medium-high heat. Fry the steaks for about 2-3 minutes on each side or until they reach the desired doneness.

3. Serve the steaks with sides of rice, fried eggs, and avocado slices.

ALBÓNDIGAS ECUATORIANAS

Ingredients

- Ground beef - 1 lb.
- Onion - 1, finely chopped.
- Garlic cloves - 2, minced.
- Cumin - 1 teaspoon.
- Coriander - 1/4 cup, chopped.
- Breadcrumbs - 1/2 cup.
- Egg - 1.
- Salt and pepper - to taste.
- Tomato sauce - 2 cups.

Instructions

1. In a bowl, mix together the ground beef, onion, garlic, cumin, coriander, breadcrumbs, egg, salt, and pepper until well combined.

2. Form the mixture into meatballs.

3. In a large skillet, cook the meatballs over medium heat until they are browned on all sides.

4. Add the tomato sauce to the skillet, cover, and simmer for about 20 minutes or until the meatballs are cooked through.

5. Serve the meatballs with sauce over cooked rice or with boiled potatoes.

PORK DISHES

Ecuadorian pork dishes embody the rich agricultural heritage and culinary diversity of the country, offering flavors that are as complex as they are comforting. These dishes are renowned for their succulence and depth, achieved through traditional cooking techniques that have been refined over generations. The fusion of indigenous spices and ingredients with pork creates a unique culinary experience, setting Ecuadorian pork cuisine apart from others with its distinct taste profiles and preparation methods.

The adaptability of pork within Ecuadorian cuisine is remarkable, allowing for a wide variety of dishes that range from slow-roasted delicacies to vibrant stews. This versatility showcases pork's ability to harmonize with a multitude of local flavors and textures, making it a staple in the Ecuadorian diet. Moreover, these pork dishes are a source of high-quality protein, vitamins, and minerals, contributing to a well-rounded and nutritious diet.

Thus, pork dishes in Ecuador are more than just meals; they are a reflection of the country's rich cultural tapestry and culinary innovation. Their significant nutritional value, paired with their unparalleled flavors, underscores the vital role of pork in Ecuadorian cuisine and its contribution to a healthy and enjoyable eating experience.

HORNADO ECUATORIANO

Ingredients

- Pork leg - 5 lbs.
- Beer - 2 cups.

- Garlic cloves - 6, minced.
- Ground cumin - 2 teaspoons.
- Salt - 3 tablespoons.
- Black pepper - 1 teaspoon.

Instructions

1. Mix the beer, garlic, cumin, salt, and pepper in a bowl to create a marinade.

2. Rub the marinade all over the pork leg. Let it marinate overnight in the refrigerator.

3. Preheat the oven to 350°F (175°C). Place the pork in a roasting pan.

4. Roast for about 4 hours, or until the pork is tender and the skin is crispy.

5. Let the pork rest before slicing. Serve with llapingachos and aji sauce.

FRITADA DE CHANCHO

Ingredients

- Pork belly - 3 lbs, cut into chunks.
- Beer - 1 cup.
- Orange juice - 1 cup.
- Garlic cloves - 4, crushed.
- Cumin - 1 teaspoon.
- Salt - 2 teaspoons.

Instructions

1. Combine the pork, beer, orange juice, garlic, cumin, and salt in a large pot.

2. Bring to a boil, then reduce heat and simmer, uncovered, for 2 hours, until the liquid evaporates and the pork fries in its own fat.

3. Turn the pork occasionally until it is golden and crispy on all sides.

4. Serve the fritada with mote pillo and aji sauce.

SECO DE CHIVO

Ingredients

- Goat meat - 3 lbs, cut into pieces (can substitute with pork for this recipe).
- Beer - 1 cup.
- Red onions - 2, chopped.
- Tomato paste - 1/4 cup.
- Garlic cloves - 4, minced.
- Ground cumin - 1 teaspoon.
- Coriander leaves - 1/2 cup, chopped.
- Orange juice - 1/2 cup.
- Salt and pepper - to taste.

Instructions

1. Marinate the meat with beer, orange juice, garlic, cumin, salt, and pepper for at least 4 hours, preferably overnight.

2. In a large pot, cook the onions until translucent. Add the marinated meat and tomato paste.

3. Cover with water and simmer for about 2 hours, until the meat is tender.

4. Add the chopped coriander before turning off the heat.

5. Serve with rice and fried plantains.

LLAPINGACHOS CON CHORIZO

Ingredients

- Potatoes - 2 lbs, boiled and mashed.
- Annatto oil - 2 tablespoons.
- Scallions - 1/2 cup, chopped.
- Chorizo - 1 lb, sliced.
- Salt and pepper - to taste.
- Cheese - 1 cup, shredded.

Instructions

1. Mix the mashed potatoes with annatto oil, scallions, salt, and pepper. Let the mixture cool.

2. Form small patties and stuff each with some cheese.

3. Fry the patties on a hot griddle or pan until golden on both sides.

4. In another pan, cook the chorizo slices until crispy.

5. Serve the llapingachos with chorizo on the side.

CHICHARRONES

Ingredients

- Pork belly - 2 lbs, cut into 1-inch pieces.
- Garlic cloves - 4, minced.
- Ground cumin - 1 teaspoon.
- Salt - 1 teaspoon.
- Water - 2 cups.

Instructions

1. In a large pot, combine pork belly, garlic, cumin, salt, and water.

2. Bring to a boil, then reduce heat to medium-low and simmer until water evaporates and pork starts to fry in its own fat, about 1 hour.

3. Continue frying the pork until it is crispy and golden brown, about 15 minutes.

4. Drain on paper towels. Serve hot with mote and aji sauce.

MOTE CON CHICHARRÓN

Ingredients

- Mote (hominy) - 2 cups, cooked.
- Pork belly - 1 lb, cut into bite-sized pieces.
- Garlic cloves - 3, minced.
- Ground cumin - 1 teaspoon.
- Salt - 1 teaspoon.
- Water - as needed for boiling pork.
- Green onions - 1/4 cup, chopped for garnish.
- Aji sauce - for serving.

Instructions

1. In a large pot, boil the pork belly with garlic, cumin, and salt until tender and water has evaporated, allowing the pork to fry in its own fat until crispy.

2. In a separate pot, cook the mote (hominy) according to package instructions until soft.

3. Serve the mote topped with the chicharrón. Garnish with green onions and serve with aji sauce on the side.

TAMALES DE CHANCHO

Ingredients

- Corn dough - 4 cups.
- Pork - 2 lbs, cooked and shredded.
- Onion - 1, diced.
- Red bell pepper - 1/2, diced.
- Garlic cloves - 3, minced.
- Cumin - 1 teaspoon.
- Achiote (annatto) oil - 2 tablespoons.
- Chicken broth - 1 cup.
- Salt and pepper - to taste.
- Banana leaves - for wrapping.

Instructions

1. Sauté the onion, red bell pepper, and garlic in achiote oil until soft. Add the shredded pork, cumin, salt, and pepper, cooking for a few more minutes.

2. Mix the pork mixture with the corn dough and gradually add chicken broth to keep it moist. Adjust seasoning as needed.

3. Cut banana leaves into squares and blanch them briefly to make them pliable. Spread a portion of the dough mixture onto a banana leaf, fold, and tie with string.

4. Steam the tamales for about 1 hour or until the dough is firm and cooked through.

5. Serve hot, removing the banana leaf before eating.

EMPANADAS DE MOROCHO CON CARNE DE CERDO

Ingredients

- Morocho (corn flour) - 2 cups.
- Pork - 1 lb, cooked and finely chopped.
- Onion - 1, finely chopped.
- Garlic cloves - 2, minced.
- Cumin - 1/2 teaspoon.
- Salt and pepper - to taste.
- Water - as needed for dough.
- Oil - for frying.

Instructions

1. Prepare the dough by mixing morocho flour with water, salt, and a bit of oil until a pliable dough forms.

2. In a pan, cook the onion, garlic, pork, cumin, salt, and pepper until well combined and flavorful.

3. Take small portions of the dough, flatten them, and fill with the pork mixture. Seal the edges to form empanadas.

4. Fry the empanadas in hot oil until golden and crispy.

5. Serve hot with a side of aji sauce.

GUATITA

Ingredients

- Tripe - 2 lbs, cleaned and cut into pieces.
- Potatoes - 3, cubed.
- Peanut paste - 1/2 cup.
- Onion - 1, chopped.

- Tomato paste - 2 tablespoons.
- Garlic cloves - 3, minced.
- Cumin - 1 teaspoon.
- Cilantro - 1/4 cup, chopped.
- Salt and pepper - to taste.
- Water - 4 cups.

Instructions

1. Boil the tripe in salted water until tender, about 2 hours. Drain and set aside.

2. In a pot, sauté onion, garlic, tomato paste, cumin, salt, and pepper until the onion is soft.

3. Add the boiled tripe, potatoes, peanut paste, and water. Simmer until the potatoes are cooked and the sauce thickens.

4. Stir in the cilantro before serving.

5. Serve hot with rice and avocado slices.

COSTILLAS DE CERDO EN SALSA DE TAMARINDO

Ingredients

- Pork ribs - 3 lbs.
- Tamarind paste - 1/4 cup.
- Brown sugar - 2 tablespoons.
- Garlic cloves - 4, minced.
- Soy sauce - 1/4 cup.
- Orange juice - 1/2 cup.
- Salt and pepper - to taste.

Instructions

1. In a bowl, mix the tamarind paste, brown sugar, garlic, soy sauce, and orange juice to create the marinade. Season with salt and pepper.

2. Marinate the pork ribs in the mixture for at least 4 hours, preferably overnight, in the refrigerator.

3. Preheat the oven to 350°F (175°C). Place the ribs in a baking dish, and cover with aluminum foil.

4. Bake for about 1.5 hours, or until the ribs are tender. Remove the foil and bake for an additional 15 minutes to caramelize the outside.

5. Serve hot, glazed with the remaining sauce.

CHANCHO AL HORNO

Ingredients

- Pork leg - 5 lbs.
- Beer - 1 cup.
- Garlic cloves - 8, minced.
- Ground cumin - 2 teaspoons.
- Orange juice - 1/2 cup.
- Soy sauce - 1/4 cup.
- Salt - 2 tablespoons.
- Black pepper - 1 teaspoon.

Instructions

1. Make a marinade by mixing beer, garlic, cumin, orange juice, soy sauce, salt, and pepper.

2. Marinate the pork leg in the mixture overnight in the

refrigerator.

3. Preheat the oven to 375°F (190°C). Place the marinated pork in a roasting pan.

4. Roast in the oven for about 4 hours, or until the meat is tender and the skin is crispy.

5. Let it rest for 15 minutes before slicing. Serve with your choice of side dishes.

CARNE AHUMADA

Ingredients

- Pork shoulder - 4 lbs.
- Wood chips - for smoking.
- Brown sugar - 1/4 cup.
- Paprika - 2 tablespoons.
- Garlic powder - 1 tablespoon.
- Salt - 2 tablespoons.
- Black pepper - 1 tablespoon.

Instructions

1. Mix brown sugar, paprika, garlic powder, salt, and pepper to create a rub.

2. Apply the rub evenly over the pork shoulder.

3. Preheat your smoker according to the manufacturer's instructions and add the wood chips.

4. Smoke the pork shoulder for about 6 hours, or until the internal temperature reaches 195°F (90°C).

5. Let the meat rest for 30 minutes before pulling or

slicing. Serve as desired.

LECHÓN ASADO

Ingredients

- Whole suckling pig - 20 lbs.
- Garlic cloves - 20, minced.
- Ground cumin - 1/4 cup.
- Oregano - 2 tablespoons.
- Orange juice - 2 cups.
- Olive oil - 1 cup.
- Salt - 1/4 cup.
- Black pepper - 2 tablespoons.

Instructions

1. Combine garlic, cumin, oregano, orange juice, olive oil, salt, and pepper to make a marinade.

2. Inject the marinade into the pig and rub it on the inside and outside. Let it marinate overnight.

3. Preheat the grill or oven to a low heat (about 325°F or 163°C).

4. Cook the pig slowly, rotating it every hour, for about 6 to 8 hours, or until the skin is crispy and the meat is tender.

5. Let it rest before carving. Serve with potatoes and salad.

MORCILLAS

Ingredients

- Pig's blood - 2 cups.
- Onion - 1, finely chopped.
- Long grain rice - 1 cup, cooked.
- Ground cumin - 1 teaspoon.
- Paprika - 1 teaspoon.
- Salt - 1 teaspoon.
- Black pepper - 1/2 teaspoon.
- Intestines - for casing.

Instructions

1. Rinse the intestines in cold water and soak in salt water for 2 hours.

2. Mix the pig's blood, onion, cooked rice, cumin, paprika, salt, and pepper in a bowl.

3. Stuff the mixture into the intestines, tying off sections to create individual sausages.

4. Boil the sausages in water for about 30 minutes, then grill or fry until the outside is crispy.

5. Serve hot with a side of potatoes and aji sauce.

PERNIL AL HORNO

Ingredients

- Pork leg - 6 lbs, skin on.
- Garlic cloves - 10, minced.
- Olive oil - 1/2 cup.
- Lemon juice - 1/4 cup.

- Orange juice - 1/2 cup.
- Ground cumin - 1 tablespoon.
- Salt - 2 tablespoons.
- Black pepper - 1 tablespoon.
- Oregano - 1 tablespoon.

Instructions

1. Preheat the oven to 350°F (175°C).

2. Make deep cuts into the pork leg. Mix together garlic, olive oil, lemon juice, orange juice, cumin, salt, pepper, and oregano to create a marinade.

3. Rub the marinade all over the pork leg, ensuring it gets into the cuts.

4. Place the pork leg in a roasting pan and cover with aluminum foil.

5. Roast in the oven for about 4 hours, or until the meat is tender. Remove the foil in the last 30 minutes to crisp the skin.

6. Let it rest before carving. Serve with your choice of side dishes.

CHICKEN DISHES

Ecuadorian chicken dishes are a testament to the country's culinary ingenuity, showcasing the versatile use of chicken in recipes that are both flavorful and deeply rooted in cultural traditions. These dishes are characterized by their tender, succulent chicken pieces, which are often marinated in a blend of local herbs and spices, then cooked to perfection. This method not only infuses the meat with rich flavors but also ensures that each dish celebrates the natural qualities of chicken, distinguishing Ecuadorian preparations from those of other cuisines.

The flexibility of chicken as an ingredient in Ecuadorian cuisine is demonstrated through an array of cooking styles, from grilling and roasting to simmering in savory stews. This versatility makes chicken a beloved protein choice across the country, capable of fitting into various meal contexts while providing essential nutrients. Chicken dishes in Ecuador are not just about taste; they also offer significant health benefits, being a great source of lean protein, vitamins, and minerals essential for a balanced diet.

Therefore, chicken dishes in Ecuador stand out for their contribution to both the country's culinary diversity and its nutritional well-being. They encapsulate the essence of Ecuadorian cooking, where healthful eating and delightful flavors coexist, enhancing the dining experience with every bite.

AJÍ DE GALLINA

Ingredients

- Chicken breast - 2 lbs, boiled and shredded.
- Bread - 4 slices, crust removed.
- Milk - 1 cup.
- Walnuts - 1/2 cup, ground.
- Ají amarillo paste - 1/4 cup.
- Onion - 1, finely chopped.
- Garlic cloves - 3, minced.
- Vegetable oil - 2 tablespoons.
- Grated Parmesan cheese - 1/4 cup.
- Chicken broth - 2 cups.
- Salt and pepper - to taste.
- Boiled eggs - 4, quartered.
- Olives - for garnish.

Instructions

1. Soak the bread in milk until soft. Blend into a smooth paste.

2. In a pot, heat the oil and sauté the onion and garlic until soft.

3. Add the ají amarillo paste and cook for a few minutes.

4. Add the bread mixture, chicken broth, ground walnuts, and shredded chicken. Cook until the sauce thickens.

5. Stir in the Parmesan cheese and season with salt and pepper.

6. Serve garnished with boiled eggs and olives.

SECO DE POLLO

Ingredients

- Chicken pieces - 2 lbs.
- Beer - 1 cup.
- Cilantro - 1 bunch, blended with a bit of water.
- Onion - 1, chopped.
- Tomato paste - 2 tablespoons.
- Garlic cloves - 4, minced.
- Cumin - 1 teaspoon.
- Orange juice - 1/2 cup.
- Vegetable oil - 2 tablespoons.
- Salt and pepper - to taste.

Instructions

1. In a large pot, heat the oil and brown the chicken pieces on all sides. Remove and set aside.

2. In the same pot, sauté the onion and garlic until soft.

3. Add the tomato paste, cumin, cilantro mixture, beer, and orange juice. Bring to a simmer.

4. Return the chicken to the pot. Cover and simmer until the chicken is tender, about 30 minutes.

5. Season with salt and pepper to taste. Serve with rice and fried plantains.

ARROZ CON POLLO

Ingredients

- Chicken pieces - 2 lbs.
- Rice - 2 cups.

- Chicken broth - 4 cups.
- Green peas - 1/2 cup.
- Carrots - 1/2 cup, diced.
- Red bell pepper - 1, diced.
- Coriander - 1/2 cup, chopped.
- Garlic cloves - 3, minced.
- Onion - 1, chopped.
- Annatto (achiote) oil - 2 tablespoons.
- Salt and pepper - to taste.

Instructions

1. In a large pot, heat the annatto oil and sauté the onion and garlic until soft.

2. Add the chicken pieces and brown on all sides.

3. Add the rice, chicken broth, green peas, carrots, and bell pepper. Bring to a boil.

4. Reduce heat to low, cover, and simmer until the rice is cooked, about 20 minutes.

5. Stir in the coriander and season with salt and pepper.

6. Serve hot.

CALDO DE GALLINA

Ingredients

- Hen - 1, cut into pieces.
- Water - 8 cups.
- Onion - 1, quartered.
- Carrots - 2, chopped.
- Celery stalks - 2, chopped.
- Garlic cloves - 2, smashed.

- Salt - to taste.
- Yucca - 1 cup, diced.
- Potatoes - 2, diced.
- Cilantro - for garnish.

Instructions

1. In a large pot, combine the hen, water, onion, carrots, celery, garlic, and salt. Bring to a boil, then reduce heat and simmer until the hen is tender, about 2 hours.

2. Add the yucca and potatoes to the pot. Continue to simmer until the vegetables are tender, about 30 minutes.

3. Adjust the seasoning as necessary. Serve hot, garnished with cilantro.

POLLO AL HORNO CON SALSA DE NARANJA

Ingredients

- Chicken pieces - 2 lbs.
- Orange juice - 1 cup.
- Garlic cloves - 4, minced.
- Soy sauce - 1/4 cup.
- Honey - 2 tablespoons.
- Olive oil - 2 tablespoons.
- Salt and pepper - to taste.
- Orange zest - from 1 orange.

Instructions

1. Preheat the oven to 375°F (190°C).

2. In a bowl, whisk together the orange juice, garlic, soy sauce, honey, olive oil, salt, pepper, and orange zest.

3. Place the chicken pieces in a baking dish and pour the orange sauce over them.

4. Bake in the preheated oven for about 45 minutes, or until the chicken is cooked through and the sauce is caramelized.

5. Serve hot, garnished with additional orange zest if desired.

ENCOCADO DE POLLO

Ingredients

- Chicken thighs - 8, skinless.
- Coconut milk - 2 cups.
- Red bell pepper - 1, sliced.
- Green bell pepper - 1, sliced.
- Onion - 1, sliced.
- Tomato - 1, chopped.
- Garlic cloves - 3, minced.
- Cumin - 1 teaspoon.
- Paprika - 1 teaspoon.
- Salt and pepper - to taste.
- Coriander - 1/4 cup, chopped.
- Lime - 1, juiced.

Instructions

1. Season the chicken thighs with salt, pepper, cumin, and paprika.

2. In a large skillet, sauté onion, garlic, red and green bell peppers until soft.

3. Add the chicken to the skillet and cook until browned on both sides.

4. Pour in the coconut milk and add the chopped tomato. Bring to a simmer.

5. Cover and cook over low heat until the chicken is cooked through, about 30 minutes.

6. Stir in lime juice and garnish with chopped coriander before serving.

POLLO A LA BRASA

Ingredients

- Whole chicken - 4 lbs.
- Soy sauce - 1/2 cup.
- Garlic cloves - 4, minced.
- Cumin - 1 teaspoon.
- Smoked paprika - 1 teaspoon.
- Black pepper - 1 teaspoon.
- Salt - 1 teaspoon.
- Olive oil - 1/4 cup.
- Beer - 1/2 cup.

Instructions

1. Mix soy sauce, garlic, cumin, smoked paprika, black pepper, salt, olive oil, and beer to create a marinade.

2. Rub the marinade all over the chicken and inside the cavity. Let marinate for at least 4 hours, preferably overnight, in the refrigerator.

3. Preheat your grill to medium-high heat. Place the chicken on the grill and cook for about 1 hour and 20 minutes, turning occasionally, until cooked through and the skin is crispy.

4. Let the chicken rest for 10 minutes before carving. Serve with your favorite side dishes.

GUISO DE POLLO

Ingredients

- Chicken pieces - 2 lbs.
- Onion - 1, chopped.
- Tomato - 2, chopped.
- Bell pepper - 1, chopped.
- Garlic cloves - 3, minced.
- Annatto (achiote) oil - 2 tablespoons.
- Potatoes - 3, cubed.
- Chicken broth - 2 cups.
- Cumin - 1 teaspoon.
- Salt and pepper - to taste.
- Cilantro - 1/4 cup, chopped for garnish.

Instructions

1. In a pot, heat the annatto oil and sauté the onion, tomato, bell pepper, and garlic until soft.

2. Add the chicken pieces and brown on all sides.

3. Add the potatoes, chicken broth, cumin, salt, and pepper. Bring to a boil, then reduce heat and simmer until the chicken is cooked through and the potatoes are tender, about 30 minutes.

4. Garnish with chopped cilantro before serving. Serve with rice or your choice of side.

POLLO SUDADO

Ingredients

- Chicken thighs - 4, skin on.
- Onion - 1, sliced.
- Tomato - 2, sliced.
- Green bell pepper - 1, sliced.
- Garlic cloves - 2, minced.
- Chicken broth - 1 cup.
- Bay leaves - 2.
- Salt and pepper - to taste.
- Olive oil - 2 tablespoons.

Instructions

1. In a large skillet, heat the olive oil over medium heat. Add the chicken thighs, skin-side down, and cook until browned. Remove and set aside.

2. In the same skillet, add the onion, tomato, green bell pepper, and garlic. Sauté until soft.

3. Return the chicken to the skillet, add chicken broth and bay leaves. Cover and simmer until the chicken is cooked through, about 30 minutes.

4. Season with salt and pepper. Serve hot with rice and avocado slices.

CUY ASADO

Ingredients

- Guinea pig (cuy) - 1, cleaned and split open.
- Garlic cloves - 5, minced.
- Ground cumin - 2 teaspoons.

- Annatto (achiote) oil - 3 tablespoons.
- Salt and pepper - to taste.
- Beer - 1/2 cup.

Instructions

1. Preheat the grill to medium-high heat.

2. Make a marinade by mixing garlic, cumin, annatto oil, salt, pepper, and beer.

3. Brush the guinea pig with the marinade and let it marinate for at least 1 hour.

4. Grill the guinea pig, turning occasionally, until the skin is crispy and the meat is cooked through, about 30 minutes to 1 hour.

5. Serve hot with potatoes and a salad.

ESTOFADO DE POLLO

Ingredients

- Chicken pieces - 2 lbs.
- Potatoes - 3, cubed.
- Carrots - 2, sliced.
- Onion - 1, chopped.
- Garlic cloves - 3, minced.
- Tomato sauce - 1 cup.
- Chicken broth - 2 cups.
- Oregano - 1 teaspoon.
- Bay leaves - 2.
- Salt and pepper - to taste.
- Olive oil - 2 tablespoons.

Instructions

1. In a large pot, heat the olive oil over medium heat. Brown the chicken pieces on all sides. Remove and set aside.

2. In the same pot, sauté the onion and garlic until soft. Add the tomato sauce, chicken broth, oregano, bay leaves, salt, and pepper.

3. Return the chicken to the pot. Add the potatoes and carrots. Bring to a boil, then reduce heat and simmer until the chicken and vegetables are tender, about 30 minutes.

4. Adjust seasoning to taste. Serve hot.

MENESTRA DE POLLO

Ingredients

- Chicken pieces - 2 lbs.
- Lentils - 1 cup, soaked overnight.
- Onion - 1, chopped.
- Green bell pepper - 1, chopped.
- Garlic cloves - 3, minced.
- Tomato paste - 2 tablespoons.
- Chicken broth - 4 cups.
- Cumin - 1 teaspoon.
- Coriander - 1/4 cup, chopped.
- Salt and pepper - to taste.
- Vegetable oil - 2 tablespoons.

Instructions

1. Heat the oil in a large pot over medium heat. Brown the chicken pieces. Remove and set aside.

2. In the same pot, sauté the onion, bell pepper, and garlic until soft. Stir in the tomato paste.

3. Add the lentils and chicken broth. Bring to a boil, then reduce heat and simmer for 20 minutes.

4. Return the chicken to the pot. Add cumin, salt, and pepper. Cook until the chicken is done and the lentils are tender, about 20 minutes more.

5. Garnish with chopped coriander. Serve hot.

POLLO CON MIEL Y MOSTAZA

Ingredients

- Chicken breasts - 4.
- Honey - 1/4 cup.
- Dijon mustard - 1/4 cup.
- Olive oil - 2 tablespoons.
- Garlic cloves - 2, minced.
- Salt and pepper - to taste.
- Lemon juice - 1 tablespoon.

Instructions

1. Preheat the oven to 375°F (190°C).

2. In a bowl, mix together the honey, mustard, olive oil, garlic, salt, pepper, and lemon juice.

3. Place the chicken breasts in a baking dish. Pour the honey mustard sauce over the chicken.

4. Bake in the preheated oven until the chicken is cooked through, about 25-30 minutes.

5. Serve hot, spooning extra sauce over the chicken.

POLLO RELLENO

Ingredients

- Whole chicken - 1.
- Ground beef - 1 lb.
- Bread crumbs - 1/2 cup.
- Milk - 1/4 cup.
- Onion - 1, chopped.
- Garlic cloves - 2, minced.
- Egg - 1.
- Raisins - 1/4 cup.
- Olives - 1/4 cup, chopped.
- Almonds - 1/4 cup, chopped.
- Salt and pepper - to taste.
- Butter - 2 tablespoons, melted.

Instructions

1. Preheat the oven to 350°F (175°C).

2. Soak the bread crumbs in milk. Mix with ground beef, onion, garlic, egg, raisins, olives, almonds, salt, and pepper to make the stuffing.

3. Stuff the chicken with the beef mixture. Sew or skewer the openings closed.

4. Place the chicken in a roasting pan. Brush with melted butter. Season with salt and pepper.

5. Roast until the chicken is cooked through and the skin is golden, about 1.5 to 2 hours. Baste occasionally with pan juices.

6. Let the chicken rest before carving. Serve with your choice of sides.

GALLINA CUYANA

Ingredients

- Hen - 1, cut into pieces.
- Onion - 2, chopped.
- Tomato - 3, chopped.
- Green bell pepper - 1, chopped.
- Garlic cloves - 4, minced.
- Potatoes - 4, cubed.
- Peas - 1 cup.
- Carrots - 2, sliced.
- Chicken broth - 4 cups.
- Oregano - 1 teaspoon.
- Bay leaf - 1.
- Salt and pepper - to taste.
- Oil - 2 tablespoons.

Instructions

1. In a large pot, heat the oil over medium heat. Brown the hen pieces on all sides. Remove and set aside.

2. In the same pot, add the onion, tomato, green bell pepper, and garlic. Cook until the vegetables are soft.

3. Return the hen to the pot. Add the potatoes, peas, carrots, chicken broth, oregano, bay leaf, salt, and pepper.

4. Bring to a boil, then reduce heat and simmer until the hen is tender and the vegetables are cooked, about 1 hour.

5. Adjust seasoning to taste. Serve hot, garnished with chopped parsley if desired.

VEGETARIAN DISHES

Ecuadorian vegetarian dishes reflect the country's rich tapestry of agricultural bounty, showcasing an array of fruits, vegetables, and grains that are central to its culinary identity. These dishes are celebrated for their vibrant flavors and textures, achieved through the inventive use of ingredients that range from the Andean highlands to the coastal plains. The meticulous preparation of vegetarian cuisine in Ecuador highlights the natural tastes and nutritional benefits of its components, setting it apart from other culinary traditions by emphasizing freshness and wholesomeness.

The versatility of vegetarian dishes in Ecuadorian cooking is noteworthy, offering a wide spectrum of options that cater to various dietary preferences and nutritional needs. From hearty quinoa salads to savory vegetable stews, the diversity of these dishes underscores Ecuador's ability to turn simple ingredients into sophisticated and nourishing meals. This adaptability not only enriches the culinary landscape but also ensures that vegetarian dishes are a source of essential nutrients, supporting a healthy lifestyle.

Thus, vegetarian cuisine in Ecuador is not merely an alternative but a fundamental aspect of the nation's gastronomic heritage. It exemplifies how a focus on plant-based ingredients can lead to meals that are both nutritionally complete and delightfully satisfying, reinforcing the importance of vegetables and grains in a balanced diet.

QUINOA CON CHAMPIÑONES

Ingredients

- Quinoa - 1 cup.
- Mushrooms - 2 cups, sliced.
- Garlic cloves - 2, minced.
- Onion - 1, diced.
- Vegetable broth - 2 cups.
- Olive oil - 2 tablespoons.
- Salt and pepper - to taste.
- Parsley - 1/4 cup, chopped for garnish.

Instructions

1. Rinse the quinoa under cold water until the water runs clear.

2. In a saucepan, heat 1 tablespoon of olive oil over medium heat. Add the onion and garlic, and sauté until soft.

3. Add the mushrooms and cook until they have released their moisture and are golden brown.

4. Add the quinoa to the saucepan, stir to combine with the mushrooms.

5. Pour in the vegetable broth and bring to a boil. Reduce heat to low, cover, and simmer for 15-20 minutes, or until the quinoa is cooked and the liquid is absorbed.

6. Season with salt and pepper. Garnish with chopped parsley before serving.

LOCRO DE ZAPALLO

Ingredients

- Butternut squash - 4 cups, cubed.
- Potatoes - 2, cubed.
- Onion - 1, chopped.
- Garlic cloves - 2, minced.
- Vegetable broth - 4 cups.
- Milk - 1 cup.
- Annatto (achiote) oil - 2 tablespoons.
- Salt and pepper - to taste.
- Queso fresco - 1/2 cup, crumbled.
- Avocado - for garnish.

Instructions

1. In a large pot, heat the annatto oil over medium heat. Add the onion and garlic, sauté until they are soft.

2. Add the butternut squash and potatoes, cook for a few minutes, stirring occasionally.

3. Pour in the vegetable broth, bring to a boil, then reduce heat and simmer until the vegetables are tender.

4. Add the milk and queso fresco, cook for another 5 minutes. Season with salt and pepper to taste.

5. Serve hot, garnished with avocado slices.

CEVICHE DE PALMITO

Ingredients

- Heart of palm - 2 cups, sliced.
- Lime juice - 1/2 cup.

- Tomato - 1, diced.
- Red onion - 1/2, thinly sliced.
- Cilantro - 1/4 cup, chopped.
- Olive oil - 2 tablespoons.
- Salt and pepper - to taste.
- Avocado - 1, diced (optional).

Instructions

1. In a mixing bowl, combine the heart of palm, lime juice, tomato, red onion, cilantro, and olive oil.

2. Season with salt and pepper to taste. Gently mix in the diced avocado, if using.

3. Let the mixture marinate in the refrigerator for at least 30 minutes to blend the flavors.

4. Serve chilled, garnished with additional cilantro if desired.

ENSALADA DE QUINUA

Ingredients

- Quinoa - 1 cup, cooked and cooled.
- Black beans - 1 cup, rinsed and drained.
- Corn - 1 cup.
- Red bell pepper - 1, diced.
- Cucumber - 1, diced.
- Red onion - 1/4 cup, finely chopped.
- Cilantro - 1/4 cup, chopped.
- Lime juice - 1/4 cup.
- Olive oil - 2 tablespoons.
- Salt and pepper - to taste.

Instructions

1. In a large bowl, combine the cooked quinoa, black beans, corn, red bell pepper, cucumber, red onion, and cilantro.

2. In a small bowl, whisk together the lime juice, olive oil, salt, and pepper.

3. Pour the dressing over the salad and toss to coat evenly.

4. Chill in the refrigerator for at least 30 minutes before serving to allow the flavors to meld.

5. Serve chilled, garnished with extra cilantro if desired.

TORTILLAS DE MAÍZ CON QUESO

Ingredients

- Corn flour (masa harina) - 2 cups.
- Water - 1 1/2 cups.
- Salt - 1 teaspoon.
- Queso fresco - 1 cup, grated.
- Butter or oil - for frying.

Instructions

1. In a large bowl, mix the corn flour, water, and salt to form a soft dough.

2. Divide the dough into small balls, then flatten each ball into a disk.

3. Place a spoonful of queso fresco in the center of each disk, fold the dough over the cheese, and press to seal,

forming a half-moon shape.

4. Heat a skillet over medium heat. Add a small amount of butter or oil.

5. Fry the tortillas until golden brown on both sides.

6. Serve hot, accompanied by a side of aji sauce.

MOTE SUCIO

Ingredients

- Mote (hominy) - 2 cups, cooked.
- Scallions - 1/4 cup, finely chopped.
- Ground peanuts - 1/2 cup.
- Cilantro - 1/4 cup, chopped.
- Hard-boiled eggs - 2, chopped.
- Salt and pepper - to taste.
- Vegetable oil - 1 tablespoon.

Instructions

1. In a large skillet, heat the oil over medium heat. Add the scallions and sauté until they are soft.

2. Add the cooked mote and ground peanuts to the skillet. Stir well to combine.

3. Cook for about 5 minutes, stirring occasionally, until the mixture is heated through.

4. Season with salt and pepper. Remove from heat and stir in the chopped cilantro.

5. Serve warm, garnished with chopped hard-boiled eggs.

ENSALADA ECUATORIANA

Ingredients

- Romaine lettuce - 4 cups, chopped.
- Tomatoes - 2, diced.
- Cucumber - 1, sliced.
- Red onion - 1/2, thinly sliced.
- Carrots - 1, shredded.
- Lime juice - 1/4 cup.
- Olive oil - 2 tablespoons.
- Salt and pepper - to taste.
- Cilantro - 1/4 cup, chopped.

Instructions

1. In a large salad bowl, combine the lettuce, tomatoes, cucumber, red onion, and carrots.

2. In a small bowl, whisk together the lime juice, olive oil, salt, and pepper to make the dressing.

3. Pour the dressing over the salad and toss to coat evenly.

4. Garnish with chopped cilantro before serving.

CHOCLO CON QUESO

Ingredients

- Corn on the cob - 4.
- Queso fresco - 1 cup, crumbled.
- Butter - 2 tablespoons, melted.
- Salt - to taste.

Instructions

1. Boil the corn in a large pot of salted water until tender, about 10 minutes.

2. Drain the corn and brush each cob with melted butter.

3. Sprinkle the crumbled queso fresco over the corn while still hot.

4. Season with salt to taste. Serve immediately.

TOSTADAS CON AGUACATE

Ingredients

- Whole wheat bread - 4 slices, toasted.
- Ripe avocados - 2, mashed.
- Lime juice - 1 tablespoon.
- Tomato - 1, diced.
- Red onion - 1/4 cup, finely chopped.
- Cilantro - 2 tablespoons, chopped.
- Salt and pepper - to taste.
- Chili flakes - 1/4 teaspoon (optional).

Instructions

1. In a bowl, mix the mashed avocados with lime juice, diced tomato, chopped red onion, cilantro, salt, and pepper. Add chili flakes if desired for extra heat.

2. Spread the avocado mixture generously over each slice of toasted bread.

3. Serve immediately, garnished with extra cilantro if desired.

EMPANADAS DE VERDE

Ingredients

- Green plantains - 3, peeled and grated.
- Queso fresco - 1 cup, crumbled.
- Salt - 1/2 teaspoon.
- Oil - for frying.

Instructions

1. In a bowl, mix the grated green plantains with salt to form a dough.

2. Take a small amount of the dough and flatten it into a circle. Place some crumbled queso fresco in the center.

3. Fold the dough over the cheese to form a half-moon shape and press the edges to seal.

4. Heat oil in a deep frying pan over medium heat. Fry the empanadas until they are golden brown on both sides.

5. Drain on paper towels. Serve hot, accompanied by aji sauce for dipping.

PATACONES CON AJO

Ingredients

- Green plantains - 2.
- Garlic cloves - 4, minced.
- Salt - 1/2 teaspoon.
- Vegetable oil - for frying.

Instructions

1. Peel the plantains and cut them into 1-inch thick slices.

2. Heat the oil in a large skillet over medium-high heat. Fry the plantain slices until they are soft and golden, about 3 minutes on each side. Remove from the skillet and drain on paper towels.

3. Flatten the fried plantains using a plantain press or the bottom of a glass bottle.

4. Mix the minced garlic with salt. Reheat the oil in the skillet over medium-high heat. Fry the flattened plantains again until they are crispy, about 2 minutes on each side. Halfway through frying, sprinkle the garlic salt mixture over the plantains.

5. Serve the patacones hot as a side dish or appetizer.

LENTEJAS ESTOFADAS

Ingredients

- Lentils - 1 cup, rinsed.
- Vegetable broth - 4 cups.
- Onion - 1, chopped.
- Carrots - 2, diced.
- Tomato - 1, diced.
- Garlic cloves - 3, minced.
- Cumin - 1 teaspoon.
- Salt and pepper - to taste.
- Olive oil - 2 tablespoons.

Instructions

1. Heat the olive oil in a large pot over medium heat. Add the onion, carrots, and garlic, sautéing until the onion is translucent.

2. Add the diced tomato and cumin, cooking for another 2 minutes.

3. Stir in the lentils and vegetable broth. Bring to a boil, then reduce heat to low and simmer, covered, until the lentils are tender, about 25-30 minutes.

4. Season with salt and pepper to taste. Serve hot, garnished with chopped cilantro if desired.

ARROZ CON MENESTRA

Ingredients

- White rice - 2 cups.
- Vegetable broth - 4 cups.
- Black beans - 1 cup, cooked.
- Onion - 1, diced.
- Red bell pepper - 1, diced.
- Garlic cloves - 3, minced.
- Cumin - 1 teaspoon.
- Salt and pepper - to taste.
- Olive oil - 2 tablespoons.

Instructions

1. In a pot, heat the olive oil over medium heat. Add the onion, red bell pepper, and garlic, sautéing until soft.

2. Add the rice, stirring to coat with the oil and vegetables. Pour in the vegetable broth, bring to a boil,

then reduce heat to low, cover, and simmer for 18-20 minutes, or until the rice is tender and the liquid is absorbed.

3. Stir in the cooked black beans, cumin, salt, and pepper. Cook for an additional 5 minutes to heat the beans through.

4. Serve hot, garnished with chopped green onions or cilantro if desired.

HUMITAS DE CHOCLO

Ingredients

- Fresh corn kernels - 4 cups.
- Butter - 1/4 cup, melted.
- Sugar - 1 tablespoon.
- Salt - 1/2 teaspoon.
- Egg - 1, beaten.
- Freshly ground black pepper - 1/4 teaspoon.
- Corn husks - soaked in water for 1 hour.

Instructions

1. Preheat the oven to 350°F (175°C).

2. In a food processor, blend the corn kernels until smooth. Transfer to a bowl and mix with melted butter, sugar, salt, beaten egg, and black pepper.

3. Drain the corn husks and pat dry. Place about 2 tablespoons of the corn mixture in the center of each husk, fold the sides over the filling, then fold the bottom up.

4. Place the humitas in a steamer and steam for about 40

minutes, or until firm and cooked through.

5. Serve hot, allowing guests to unwrap their own humitas.

PASTEL DE CHOCLO

Ingredients

- Fresh corn kernels - 6 cups.
- Milk - 1 cup.
- Butter - 1/4 cup.
- Sugar - 2 tablespoons.
- Salt - 1 teaspoon.
- Fresh basil - 1/4 cup, chopped.
- Hard-boiled eggs - 4, sliced.
- Queso fresco - 1 cup, crumbled.

Instructions

1. Preheat the oven to 375°F (190°C).

2. In a blender, puree the corn kernels with milk until smooth.

3. In a large skillet, melt the butter over medium heat. Add the corn puree, sugar, and salt. Cook, stirring constantly, until the mixture thickens, about 10 minutes. Remove from heat and stir in the chopped basil.

4. In a greased baking dish, layer half of the corn mixture, followed by a layer of sliced hard-boiled eggs and crumbled queso fresco. Cover with the remaining corn mixture.

5. Bake in the preheated oven for about 30 minutes, or until the top is golden and set. 6. Serve hot.

RICE DISHES

Ecuadorian rice dishes are a culinary staple, embodying the essence of the nation's gastronomy through the versatile and creative use of rice as a central ingredient. These dishes are renowned for their ability to marry a variety of local flavors, incorporating seafood, meat, vegetables, and spices into the rice, which absorbs and enhances these elements. The technique and care in preparation showcase the cultural significance of rice in Ecuador, differentiating it from other global rice traditions by emphasizing its role in both everyday meals and festive occasions.

The adaptability of rice in Ecuadorian cuisine is evident in the broad spectrum of dishes available, from comforting bowls of arroz con pollo (chicken and rice) to the coastal favorite, arroz con camarones (rice with shrimp). This flexibility demonstrates rice's capacity to serve as a nutritious base for a multitude of ingredients, catering to a wide range of tastes and dietary preferences. Furthermore, these rice dishes are not only rich in flavor but also offer a balance of essential nutrients, providing a foundation for healthy eating.

Therefore, rice dishes in Ecuador stand as a testament to the country's rich agricultural heritage and culinary creativity. They highlight the importance of rice as a nourishing and unifying element in Ecuadorian cuisine, capable of bringing together diverse ingredients in a harmonious and healthful way.

ARROZ CON CAMARÓN

Ingredients

- Shrimp - 2 lbs, peeled and deveined.
- White rice - 2 cups.
- Vegetable broth - 4 cups.
- Onion - 1, finely chopped.
- Red bell pepper - 1, diced.
- Garlic cloves - 3, minced.
- Tomato paste - 2 tablespoons.
- Peas - 1/2 cup.
- Carrots - 1/2 cup, diced.
- Annatto (achiote) oil - 2 tablespoons.
- Cilantro - 1/4 cup, chopped.
- Salt and pepper - to taste.

Instructions

1. In a large skillet, heat the annatto oil over medium heat. Add the onion, red bell pepper, and garlic. Sauté until the onion is translucent.

2. Stir in the tomato paste and cook for another 2 minutes.

3. Add the rice, stirring to coat with the vegetable mixture. Pour in the vegetable broth. Bring to a boil, then reduce heat to low, cover, and simmer for 15 minutes.

4. Add the shrimp, peas, and carrots. Cover and cook for an additional 10 minutes, or until the shrimp are pink and the rice is tender.

5. Season with salt and pepper. Garnish with chopped cilantro before serving.

ARROZ CON POLLO

Ingredients

- Chicken pieces - 2 lbs.
- White rice - 2 cups.
- Chicken broth - 4 cups.
- Onion - 1, chopped.
- Green bell pepper - 1, chopped.
- Garlic cloves - 4, minced.
- Tomato sauce - 1 cup.
- Peas - 1/2 cup.
- Carrots - 1/2 cup, diced.
- Cumin - 1 teaspoon.
- Coriander - 1/4 cup, chopped.
- Annatto (achiote) oil - 2 tablespoons.
- Salt and pepper - to taste.

Instructions

1. In a large pot, heat the annatto oil over medium heat. Add the chicken pieces and brown on all sides. Remove and set aside.

2. In the same pot, add the onion, green bell pepper, and garlic. Cook until soft.

3. Stir in the tomato sauce, cumin, and rice. Cook for 2 minutes, stirring frequently.

4. Add the chicken broth and bring to a boil. Return the chicken to the pot, then add the peas and carrots.

5. Reduce heat to low, cover, and simmer for 20-25 minutes, or until the rice is cooked and the chicken is tender.

6. Season with salt and pepper. Garnish with chopped coriander before serving.

ARROZ CON MENESTRA Y CARNE ASADA

Ingredients

- Beef - 2 lbs, thinly sliced.
- White rice - 2 cups.
- Lentils - 1 cup, cooked.
- Beef broth - 4 cups.
- Onion - 1, chopped.
- Garlic cloves - 3, minced.
- Red bell pepper - 1, chopped.
- Ground cumin - 1 teaspoon.
- Annatto (achiote) oil - 2 tablespoons.
- Salt and pepper - to taste.

Instructions

1. Season the beef slices with salt, pepper, and cumin. Grill or pan-fry until cooked to your liking. Set aside and keep warm.

2. In a large pot, heat the annatto oil over medium heat. Add the onion, garlic, and red bell pepper. Cook until the onion is soft.

3. Add the rice and stir to coat with the oil and vegetables. Pour in the beef broth. Bring to a boil, then reduce heat to low, cover, and simmer for 18 minutes.

4. Stir in the cooked lentils and heat through.

5. Serve the rice and lentils with the grilled beef on the side.

ARROZ MARINERO

Ingredients

- Mixed seafood (shrimp, squid, mussels) - 2 lbs.
- White rice - 2 cups.
- Vegetable broth - 4 cups.
- Onion - 1, chopped.
- Red bell pepper - 1, chopped.
- Garlic cloves - 3, minced.
- Tomato paste - 1/4 cup.
- Peas - 1/2 cup.
- Annatto (achiote) oil - 2 tablespoons.
- Cilantro - 1/4 cup, chopped.
- Salt and pepper - to taste.

Instructions

1. In a large pot, heat the annatto oil over medium heat. Add the onion, red bell pepper, and garlic. Cook until the onion is translucent.

2. Stir in the tomato paste and rice. Cook for 2 minutes, stirring frequently.

3. Add the vegetable broth and bring to a boil. Reduce heat to low, cover, and simmer for 15 minutes.

4. Add the mixed seafood and peas. Cook for an additional 5 minutes, or until the seafood is cooked through.

5. Season with salt and pepper. Garnish with chopped cilantro before serving.

ARROZ CON CALAMARES

Ingredients

- Squid - 2 lbs, cleaned and sliced.
- White rice - 2 cups.
- Fish broth - 4 cups.
- Onion - 1, chopped.
- Garlic cloves - 3, minced.
- Tomato sauce - 1/2 cup.
- Peas - 1/2 cup.
- Red bell pepper - 1, diced.
- Paprika - 1 teaspoon.
- Annatto (achiote) oil - 2 tablespoons.
- Salt and pepper - to taste.

Instructions

1. In a large pot, heat the annatto oil over medium heat. Add the onion and garlic. Cook until soft.

2. Add the squid and cook for 2-3 minutes.

3. Stir in the tomato sauce and paprika. Cook for another 2 minutes.

4. Add the rice, stirring to coat it with the sauce. Pour in the fish broth. Bring to a boil, then reduce heat to low, cover, and simmer for 18 minutes.

5. Stir in the peas and red bell pepper. Cook for an additional 5 minutes, or until the rice is tender and the liquid is absorbed.

6. Season with salt and pepper before serving.

ARROZ CON CHORIZO

Ingredients

- White rice - 2 cups.
- Chorizo - 1 cup, sliced.
- Onion - 1, diced.
- Garlic cloves - 2, minced.
- Chicken broth - 4 cups.
- Peas - 1/2 cup.
- Carrots - 1/2 cup, diced.
- Annatto (achiote) oil - 2 tablespoons.
- Salt and pepper - to taste.

Instructions

1. In a large pan, heat the annatto oil over medium heat. Add the chorizo and cook until browned. Remove the chorizo and set aside.

2. In the same pan, add the onion and garlic. Sauté until the onion is translucent.

3. Add the rice, stirring constantly for about 2 minutes.

4. Pour in the chicken broth and bring to a boil. Reduce heat to low, cover, and simmer for 20 minutes, or until the rice is tender.

5. Add the cooked chorizo, peas, and carrots. Cook for an additional 5 minutes.

6. Season with salt and pepper to taste. Serve hot.

ARROZ CON COCO

Ingredients

- White rice - 2 cups.
- Coconut milk - 4 cups.
- Sugar - 1/4 cup.
- Salt - 1 teaspoon.
- Grated coconut - 1/2 cup (optional for garnish).

Instructions

1. In a pot, bring the coconut milk to a boil. Add the sugar and salt, stirring until dissolved.

2. Add the rice to the pot and reduce heat to low. Cover and simmer for 20-25 minutes, or until the rice is tender and the liquid is absorbed.

3. Fluff the rice with a fork and serve hot, garnished with grated coconut if desired.

ARROZ CON GUANDULES

Ingredients

- White rice - 2 cups.
- Pigeon peas (guandules) - 1 cup, canned or cooked.
- Onion - 1, chopped.
- Garlic cloves - 2, minced.
- Chicken broth - 4 cups.
- Tomato paste - 2 tablespoons.
- Annatto (achiote) oil - 2 tablespoons.
- Cumin - 1 teaspoon.
- Salt and pepper - to taste.

Instructions

1. In a large pot, heat the annatto oil over medium heat. Add the onion and garlic, cooking until the onion is soft.

2. Stir in the tomato paste, cumin, and rice. Cook for about 2 minutes.

3. Add the pigeon peas and chicken broth. Bring to a boil, then reduce heat to low. Cover and simmer for 20 minutes, or until the rice is tender.

4. Season with salt and pepper to taste. Serve hot.

ARROZ TÍPICO ECUATORIANO

Ingredients

- White rice - 2 cups.
- Annatto (achiote) oil - 2 tablespoons.
- Onion - 1, finely chopped.
- Red bell pepper - 1, diced.
- Garlic cloves - 3, minced.
- Tomato sauce - 1/2 cup.
- Chicken broth - 4 cups.
- Peas - 1/2 cup.
- Carrots - 1/2 cup, diced.
- Salt and pepper - to taste.

Instructions

1. In a large pot, heat the annatto oil over medium heat. Add the onion, red bell pepper, and garlic. Sauté until the onion is translucent.

2. Stir in the tomato sauce and then the rice, making sure the rice is well coated with the sauce.

3. Add the chicken broth and bring to a boil. Reduce the heat to low, cover, and simmer for 20 minutes.

4. Add the peas and carrots, cook for an additional 5 minutes.

5. Season with salt and pepper. Serve hot.

RISOTTO DE QUINOA

Ingredients

- Quinoa - 1 cup, rinsed.
- Vegetable broth - 4 cups.
- White wine - 1/2 cup.
- Onion - 1, finely chopped.
- Garlic cloves - 2, minced.
- Mushrooms - 1 cup, sliced.
- Butter - 2 tablespoons.
- Parmesan cheese - 1/2 cup, grated.
- Salt and pepper - to taste.
- Parsley - for garnish.

Instructions

1. In a large saucepan, melt the butter over medium heat. Add the onion and garlic, sautéing until soft.

2. Add the quinoa and cook, stirring constantly, for about 2 minutes.

3. Pour in the white wine and cook until it has been absorbed by the quinoa.

4. Add the vegetable broth, one cup at a time, waiting until each addition is absorbed before adding the next.

5. When the quinoa is cooked and creamy, stir in the mushrooms and cook for an additional 5 minutes.

6. Remove from heat, stir in the Parmesan cheese, and season with salt and pepper.

7. Serve garnished with parsley.

ARROZ VERDE

Ingredients

- White rice - 2 cups.
- Spinach - 1 cup, packed.
- Cilantro - 1/2 cup, packed.
- Chicken or vegetable broth - 4 cups.
- Garlic cloves - 2, minced.
- Onion - 1, chopped.
- Green bell pepper - 1, diced.
- Olive oil - 2 tablespoons.
- Salt and pepper - to taste.

Instructions

1. In a blender, puree the spinach, cilantro, and broth until smooth.

2. In a large pot, heat the olive oil over medium heat. Add the garlic, onion, and green bell pepper. Sauté until the onion is translucent.

3. Add the rice, stirring to coat with the oil and vegetables. Cook for about 2 minutes.

4. Pour in the green broth mixture. Bring to a boil, then reduce heat to low, cover, and simmer for 20 minutes, or until the rice is tender and the liquid is absorbed.

5. Season with salt and pepper to taste. Fluff with a fork before serving.

ARROZ CON CHAMPIÑONES

Ingredients

- White rice - 2 cups.
- Mushrooms - 2 cups, sliced.
- Chicken or vegetable broth - 4 cups.
- Garlic cloves - 3, minced.
- Onion - 1, chopped.
- Butter - 2 tablespoons.
- Olive oil - 1 tablespoon.
- Salt and pepper - to taste.
- Parsley - 1/4 cup, chopped for garnish.

Instructions

1. In a large pan, heat the olive oil and butter over medium heat. Add the onion and garlic. Cook until the onion is soft.

2. Add the mushrooms and sauté until they are browned and have released their moisture.

3. Stir in the rice until well coated with the mushroom mixture.

4. Pour in the broth and bring to a boil. Reduce heat to low, cover, and simmer for 20 minutes, or until the rice is tender and the liquid is absorbed.

5. Season with salt and pepper. Garnish with parsley before serving.

ARROZ CON PATO

Ingredients

- Duck - 1, cut into pieces.
- White rice - 2 cups.
- Beer - 1 cup.
- Chicken broth - 3 cups.
- Onion - 1, chopped.
- Garlic cloves - 4, minced.
- Red bell pepper - 1, diced.
- Cilantro - 1/2 cup, chopped.
- Annatto (achiote) oil - 2 tablespoons.
- Cumin - 1 teaspoon.
- Salt and pepper - to taste.

Instructions

1. Season the duck pieces with salt, pepper, and cumin. In a large pot, heat the annatto oil over medium heat. Add the duck and brown on all sides. Remove and set aside.

2. In the same pot, add the onion, garlic, and red bell pepper. Cook until the onion is translucent.

3. Add the rice and cilantro, stirring until the rice is well coated with the oil and vegetables.

4. Pour in the beer and chicken broth. Return the duck to the pot. Bring to a boil, then reduce heat to low, cover, and simmer for 30 minutes, or until the rice is tender and the duck is cooked through.

5. Adjust seasoning if necessary. Serve hot, garnished with additional chopped cilantro.

ARROZ CON LECHE
(DESSERT VERSION)

Ingredients

- White rice - 1 cup.
- Milk - 4 cups.
- Sugar - 1 cup.
- Cinnamon stick - 1.
- Condensed milk - 1/2 cup.
- Raisins - 1/2 cup.
- Lemon zest - 1 teaspoon.
- Ground cinnamon - for garnish.

Instructions

1. In a large pot, combine the rice, milk, and cinnamon stick. Bring to a boil, then reduce heat to low and simmer, stirring occasionally, until the rice is tender, about 20 minutes.

2. Add the sugar, condensed milk, and raisins. Continue to simmer, stirring frequently, until the mixture thickens, about 10 minutes.

3. Remove from heat and stir in the lemon zest.

4. Discard the cinnamon stick. Serve warm or chilled, garnished with ground cinnamon.

ARROZ NEGRO

Ingredients

- White rice - 2 cups.
- Squid ink - 2 sachets.
- Chicken or fish broth - 4 cups.

- Onion - 1, chopped.
- Garlic cloves - 3, minced.
- Squid - 1 cup, sliced.
- Olive oil - 2 tablespoons.
- Salt and pepper - to taste.
- Lemon wedges - for serving.

Instructions

1. In a large pan, heat the olive oil over medium heat. Add the onion and garlic, cooking until soft.

2. Add the squid and cook for about 2 minutes, or until it starts to turn opaque.

3. Stir in the rice until well coated with the oil and squid mixture.

4. Mix the squid ink with the broth and add to the pan. Bring to a boil, then reduce heat to low, cover, and simmer for 20 minutes, or until the rice is tender and the liquid is absorbed.

5. Season with salt and pepper. Serve hot with lemon wedges on the side.

SAUCES

Ecuadorian sauces are pivotal in defining the flavor profile of the country's cuisine, serving as a vibrant testament to its culinary diversity and ingenuity. These sauces, crafted from a rich palette of local herbs, spices, fruits, and vegetables, imbue dishes with depth and complexity. Their uniqueness lies in the meticulous blending of ingredients, which captures the essence of Ecuadorian biodiversity, setting these condiments apart from others by enriching meals with distinctive flavors and aromas.

The versatility of Ecuadorian sauces is remarkable, with each type serving a specific purpose, whether it's enhancing the main dish, adding moisture, or providing a spicy kick. This adaptability underscores their role in complementing a wide range of dishes, from traditional meats and seafood to vegetarian options. Moreover, these sauces are not just about flavor; they also contribute nutritional value, including vitamins and antioxidants, thanks to the fresh, whole ingredients used in their preparation.

Therefore, sauces in Ecuadorian cuisine are more than mere accompaniments; they are essential components that complete and elevate the dining experience. Their nutritional benefits and flavor-enhancing properties underscore the importance of sauces in creating balanced, healthful, and delicious meals.

AJI CRIOLLO

Ingredients

- Hot peppers (aji) - 10, seeded and chopped.

- Cilantro - 1/2 cup, chopped.
- Green onions - 1/4 cup, chopped.
- Garlic cloves - 2, minced.
- Lime juice - 1/4 cup.
- Water - 1/4 cup.
- Salt - to taste.

Instructions

1. Combine the hot peppers, cilantro, green onions, and garlic in a blender or food processor.

2. Add the lime juice and water. Blend until smooth.

3. Season with salt to taste. Adjust the consistency by adding more water if necessary.

4. Serve as a condiment with your favorite Ecuadorian dishes.

SALSA DE MANÍ

Ingredients

- Peanut butter - 1/2 cup.
- Onion - 1/4 cup, finely chopped.
- Garlic clove - 1, minced.
- Milk - 1 cup.
- Cilantro - 2 tablespoons, chopped.
- Salt and pepper - to taste.
- Vegetable oil - 1 tablespoon.

Instructions

1. Heat the oil in a saucepan over medium heat. Add the onion and garlic, cooking until they are soft and fragrant.

2. Stir in the peanut butter and milk, whisking until smooth.

3. Cook over low heat, stirring constantly, until the sauce thickens, about 5 minutes.

4. Add the chopped cilantro and season with salt and pepper to taste.

5. Serve warm with dishes such as llapingachos or seco de pollo.

SALSA VERDE

Ingredients

- Tomatillos - 1 lb, husked and washed.
- Jalapeños - 2, seeded and chopped.
- Onion - 1/2, chopped.
- Garlic cloves - 2, minced.
- Cilantro - 1/2 cup, chopped.
- Lime juice - 2 tablespoons.
- Salt - to taste.
- Water - as needed.

Instructions

1. Boil the tomatillos and jalapeños in water until soft, about 10 minutes. Drain.

2. In a blender, combine the boiled tomatillos, jalapeños, onion, garlic, cilantro, and lime juice. Blend until smooth.

3. If the sauce is too thick, add a little water to reach the desired consistency.

4. Season with salt to taste. Serve with chips or as a

topping for your favorite dishes.

SALSA DE TOMATE CRIOLLA

Ingredients

- Ripe tomatoes - 4, diced.
- Red onion - 1/2, finely chopped.
- Lime juice - 2 tablespoons.
- Cilantro - 1/4 cup, chopped.
- Salt and pepper - to taste.

Instructions

1. In a bowl, combine the diced tomatoes, chopped red onion, lime juice, and chopped cilantro.

2. Season with salt and pepper to taste. Mix well.

3. Let the salsa sit for at least 10 minutes to allow the flavors to meld together.

4. Serve as a refreshing side or topping for meats and other dishes.

CHIMICHURRI ECUATORIANO

Ingredients

- Parsley - 1 cup, chopped.
- Garlic cloves - 3, minced.
- Oregano - 2 teaspoons, dried.
- Red wine vinegar - 1/4 cup.
- Olive oil - 1/2 cup.
- Red chili flakes - 1 teaspoon.
- Salt and pepper - to taste.

Instructions

1. In a bowl, combine the chopped parsley, minced garlic, dried oregano, red wine vinegar, olive oil, and red chili flakes.

2. Season with salt and pepper to taste. Whisk until well combined.

3. Let the chimichurri sauce sit for at least 30 minutes before serving to allow the flavors to develop.

4. Serve as a condiment with grilled meats or as a dressing for salads.

SALSA ROSADA

Ingredients

- Mayonnaise - 1/2 cup.
- Ketchup - 1/4 cup.
- Lime juice - 1 tablespoon.
- Worcestershire sauce - 1 teaspoon.
- Hot sauce - to taste (optional).
- Salt and pepper - to taste.

Instructions

1. In a bowl, combine mayonnaise, ketchup, lime juice, Worcestershire sauce, and hot sauce (if using).

2. Mix well until all the ingredients are fully integrated.

3. Season with salt and pepper to taste.

4. Serve chilled as a dip or sauce for seafood, fried foods, or as a dressing for salads.

SALSA DE AJO

Ingredients

- Garlic cloves - 8, minced.
- Olive oil - 1/2 cup.
- Lemon juice - 3 tablespoons.
- Egg yolk - 1 (optional for creaminess).
- Salt - to taste.

Instructions

1. In a blender or food processor, combine the minced garlic, olive oil, lemon juice, and egg yolk (if using).

2. Blend until the mixture becomes smooth and creamy.

3. Season with salt to taste.

4. Serve as a condiment with grilled meats, seafood, or as a spread for bread.

SALSA DE CILANTRO

Ingredients

- Cilantro - 1 cup, packed.
- Yogurt or sour cream - 1/2 cup.
- Lime juice - 2 tablespoons.
- Garlic clove - 1, minced.
- Olive oil - 2 tablespoons.
- Salt and pepper - to taste.

Instructions

1. In a blender or food processor, combine cilantro, yogurt or sour cream, lime juice, minced garlic, and olive oil.

2. Blend until the mixture is smooth.

3. Season with salt and pepper to taste.

4. Serve as a sauce or dressing for salads, grilled vegetables, or as a dip.

ENCURTIDO
(PICKLED ONIONS AND TOMATOES)

Ingredients

- Red onions - 2, thinly sliced.
- Tomatoes - 2, thinly sliced.
- Lime juice - 1/4 cup.
- Orange juice - 1/4 cup.
- White vinegar - 1/4 cup.
- Sugar - 1 teaspoon.
- Salt - 1 teaspoon.
- Cilantro - 1/4 cup, chopped.

Instructions

1. In a bowl, combine lime juice, orange juice, vinegar, sugar, and salt. Stir until the sugar and salt are dissolved.

2. Add the thinly sliced onions and tomatoes to the mixture. Let them marinate for at least 30 minutes, stirring occasionally.

3. Before serving, stir in the chopped cilantro.

4. Serve as a garnish or accompaniment to dishes such as ceviches, grilled meats, or seafood.

SALSA DE TAMARINDO

Ingredients

- Tamarind paste - 1/4 cup.
- Water - 1 cup.
- Sugar - 1/2 cup (adjust to taste).
- Soy sauce - 2 tablespoons.
- Garlic clove - 1, minced.
- Salt - 1/2 teaspoon.
- Red chili flakes - 1/2 teaspoon (optional for heat).

Instructions

1. In a small saucepan, combine the tamarind paste and water. Heat over medium heat, stirring until the paste has dissolved.

2. Add the sugar, soy sauce, minced garlic, salt, and red chili flakes (if using). Cook, stirring occasionally, until the mixture thickens into a sauce, about 10-15 minutes.

3. Adjust the sweetness or saltiness to your taste. Let the sauce cool down.

4. Serve as a dipping sauce for snacks, appetizers, or use it to glaze meats and vegetables.

BREADS

Ecuadorian breads are a fundamental aspect of the country's culinary tradition, showcasing an array of unique types and flavors that reflect the diversity of its regions and cultures. These breads are distinguished by their use of local ingredients, such as corn, yuca, and various grains, which contribute to their distinct textures and tastes. The art of bread-making in Ecuador is a testament to its rich cultural heritage, with each variety offering a glimpse into the local customs and dietary preferences, setting them apart from bread traditions elsewhere.

The versatility of Ecuadorian bread is evident in its many forms, from sweet to savory, soft to crusty, each suited to different times of the day and types of meals. This adaptability makes Ecuadorian bread a staple in both daily diets and special celebrations, capable of complementing a wide range of dishes or being enjoyed on its own. Beyond their versatility, these breads are a source of essential nutrients, providing energy and sustenance through whole grains and enriched flours.

Thus, Ecuadorian breads play a crucial role in the country's gastronomy, not just as an accompaniment but as a beloved element of meals that carries both cultural significance and nutritional value. Their rich variety and healthful qualities make them an integral part of Ecuadorian cuisine, celebrated for their ability to bring people together and nourish the body.

PAN DE YUCA

Ingredients

- Yuca flour - 2 cups.
- Queso fresco - 1 cup, crumbled.
- Eggs - 2.
- Baking powder - 1 teaspoon.
- Butter - 2 tablespoons, melted.
- Salt - 1/2 teaspoon.

Instructions

1. Preheat the oven to 350°F (175°C) and line a baking sheet with parchment paper.

2. In a large bowl, mix the yuca flour, crumbled queso fresco, baking powder, and salt.

3. Add the eggs and melted butter to the dry ingredients. Mix until a dough forms. If the dough is too dry, add a little milk (one tablespoon at a time) until it comes together.

4. Take small portions of the dough and roll them into balls. Place the balls on the prepared baking sheet.

5. Bake for 20-25 minutes, or until they are golden and puffed up.

6. Serve warm. Pan de yuca is best enjoyed fresh out of the oven.

PAN DE MAÍZ

Ingredients

- Cornmeal - 2 cups.
- Flour - 1 cup.
- Sugar - 1/2 cup.
- Milk - 2 cups.
- Eggs - 2.
- Baking powder - 1 tablespoon.
- Salt - 1 teaspoon.
- Butter - 1/2 cup, melted.

Instructions

1. Preheat the oven to 375°F (190°C) and grease a baking pan.

2. In a large bowl, combine the cornmeal, flour, sugar, baking powder, and salt.

3. In another bowl, beat the eggs with the milk and melted butter.

4. Add the wet ingredients to the dry ingredients and mix until just combined.

5. Pour the batter into the prepared baking pan.

6. Bake for 30-35 minutes, or until a toothpick inserted into the center comes out clean.

7. Let cool before slicing. Serve the pan de maíz as a side dish or enjoy it as a snack.

PAN DE QUESO

Ingredients

- Tapioca flour - 2 cups.
- Mozzarella cheese - 1 cup, shredded.
- Queso fresco - 1 cup, crumbled.
- Milk - 1/2 cup.
- Eggs - 2.
- Butter - 1/4 cup, melted.
- Salt - 1/2 teaspoon.

Instructions

1. Preheat the oven to 400°F (200°C) and line a baking sheet with parchment paper.

2. In a large bowl, combine the tapioca flour and salt. Add the shredded mozzarella, crumbled queso fresco, milk, eggs, and melted butter.

3. Mix until a sticky dough forms. If the dough is too sticky, add a bit more tapioca flour.

4. With oiled hands, form the dough into small balls and place them on the prepared baking sheet.

5. Bake for 15-20 minutes, or until the bread is puffed and lightly golden.

6. Serve warm. Pan de queso is best enjoyed fresh from the oven.

ROSCAS

Ingredients

- Flour - 4 cups.
- Sugar - 1 cup.
- Butter - 1/2 cup, room temperature.
- Eggs - 2.
- Milk - 1 cup, warm.
- Yeast - 1 tablespoon, active dry.
- Salt - 1 teaspoon.
- Anise seeds - 1 teaspoon.
- Egg wash - 1 egg beaten with 1 tablespoon of water.

Instructions

1. Dissolve the yeast in the warm milk with a teaspoon of sugar. Let it sit for 5-10 minutes until frothy.

2. In a large mixing bowl, combine the flour, the rest of the sugar, salt, and anise seeds.

3. Add the butter, eggs, and the yeast mixture. Mix until a dough forms.

4. Knead the dough on a floured surface for about 10 minutes, until smooth and elastic.

5. Place the dough in a greased bowl, cover with a damp cloth, and let it rise in a warm place for about 1 hour, or until doubled in size.

6. Punch down the dough and divide it into pieces. Roll each piece into a long rope and form a circle, pressing the ends together to seal.

7. Place the roscas on a baking sheet lined with

parchment paper. Brush with egg wash.

8. Preheat the oven to 350°F (175°C) and bake for 20-25 minutes, or until golden brown.

9. Let cool on a wire rack before serving.

BIZCOCHOS DE CAYAMBE

Ingredients

- Flour - 3 cups.
- Butter - 1 cup, cold and cubed.
- Sugar - 1/2 cup.
- Eggs - 1, for dough plus 1 for glazing.
- Salt - 1/2 teaspoon.
- Baking powder - 1 teaspoon.
- Milk - as needed.

Instructions

1. Preheat the oven to 375°F (190°C) and line a baking sheet with parchment paper.

2. In a large bowl, mix the flour, sugar, salt, and baking powder.

3. Add the cold, cubed butter to the flour mixture. Use your fingertips to rub the butter into the flour until the mixture resembles coarse crumbs.

4. Beat 1 egg and add to the mixture. Gradually add milk, a tablespoon at a time, kneading until a firm dough forms.

5. Roll out the dough on a floured surface to about 1/4 inch thick. Cut into desired shapes with a cookie cutter.

6. Place the bizcochos on the prepared baking sheet. Beat the remaining egg and brush over the top of each bizcocho.

7. Bake for 15-20 minutes, or until golden brown.

8. Serve warm or at room temperature, ideally with hot chocolate or coffee.

PAN DE ALMIDÓN

Ingredients

- Tapioca starch (almidón de yuca) - 2 cups.
- Eggs - 3.
- Butter - 1/2 cup, melted.
- Queso fresco - 1 cup, crumbled.
- Salt - 1/2 teaspoon.

Instructions

1. Preheat the oven to 350°F (175°C) and grease a baking sheet or line it with parchment paper.

2. In a large bowl, combine the tapioca starch and salt. Add the eggs, melted butter, and queso fresco, mixing until a smooth dough forms.

3. Roll the dough into small balls, about the size of a golf ball, and place them on the prepared baking sheet.

4. Bake for 15-20 minutes, or until the breads are puffed up and lightly golden.

5. Serve warm. Pan de almidón is best enjoyed fresh from the oven.

GUAGUAS DE PAN

Ingredients

- All-purpose flour - 4 cups.
- Granulated sugar - 1/2 cup.
- Butter - 1/2 cup, softened.
- Eggs - 2.
- Milk - 1 cup, lukewarm.
- Active dry yeast - 1 tablespoon.
- Salt - 1 teaspoon.
- Anise seeds - 1 teaspoon.
- Raisins - for decoration.

Instructions

1. Dissolve the yeast in the lukewarm milk with a teaspoon of sugar. Let it sit for about 10 minutes until frothy.

2. In a large mixing bowl, combine the flour, the remaining sugar, salt, and anise seeds.

3. Add the softened butter, eggs, and yeast mixture to the flour. Mix until a dough forms.

4. Knead the dough on a floured surface for about 10 minutes until smooth and elastic.

5. Place the dough in a greased bowl, cover with a damp cloth, and let it rise in a warm place for about 1 hour, or until doubled in size.

6. Punch down the dough and divide it into portions. Shape each portion into a "guagua" (baby) shape. Use raisins to decorate for eyes and buttons.

7. Preheat the oven to 375°F (190°C). Place the shaped dough on a baking sheet lined with parchment paper and let them rise again for about 30 minutes.

8. Bake for 20-25 minutes, or until golden brown.

9. Let the guaguas de pan cool on a wire rack before serving.

PAN DE PINLLO

Ingredients

- Whole wheat flour - 3 cups.
- Water - 1 cup, warm.
- Active dry yeast - 1 tablespoon.
- Sugar - 2 tablespoons.
- Salt - 1 teaspoon.
- Butter - 2 tablespoons, melted.

Instructions

1. Dissolve the yeast and sugar in the warm water. Let it sit for about 10 minutes until frothy.

2. In a large bowl, mix the whole wheat flour and salt. Add the yeast mixture and melted butter. Mix until a dough forms.

3. Knead the dough on a floured surface for about 10 minutes until smooth and elastic.

4. Place the dough in a greased bowl, cover with a damp cloth, and let it rise in a warm place for 1 hour, or until doubled in size.

5. Punch down the dough and shape it into loaves or

rolls. Place them on a baking sheet lined with parchment paper.

6. Preheat the oven to 375°F (190°C). Let the dough rise again for about 30 minutes.

7. Bake for 25-30 minutes, or until the bread sounds hollow when tapped on the bottom.

8. Let the bread cool on a wire rack before slicing.

TORTILLAS DE TRIGO

Ingredients

- All-purpose flour - 2 cups.
- Water - 3/4 cup, warm.
- Salt - 1 teaspoon.
- Vegetable oil - 2 tablespoons.

Instructions

1. In a large bowl, mix the flour and salt. Add the vegetable oil and warm water, mixing until a dough forms.

2. Knead the dough on a floured surface for about 5 minutes until it's smooth and elastic.

3. Divide the dough into small balls, about the size of a golf ball. Roll each ball out on a floured surface to a thin circle.

4. Heat a skillet over medium-high heat. Cook each tortilla for about 1 minute on each side, or until it starts to show brown spots.

5. Keep the tortillas warm by wrapping them in a clean cloth until ready to serve.

BOLLOS DE MAÍZ

Ingredients

- Cornmeal - 2 cups.
- Water - 2 cups, warm.
- Sugar - 1/4 cup.
- Salt - 1/2 teaspoon.
- Butter - 2 tablespoons, melted.
- Queso fresco - 1 cup, crumbled (optional).

Instructions

1. In a large bowl, mix the cornmeal, sugar, and salt. Add the warm water and melted butter, mixing until a thick batter forms. If using, fold in the crumbled queso fresco.

2. Let the batter rest for 10 minutes to thicken further.

3. Preheat the oven to 350°F (175°C) and grease a muffin tin or prepare corn husks for wrapping.

4. Fill the muffin tins or corn husks with the batter.

5. Bake for 25-30 minutes if using a muffin tin, or steam for about an hour if using corn husks, until the bollos are cooked through.

6. Serve warm. Bollos de maíz can be enjoyed as a breakfast dish or a snack.

DESSERTS

Ecuadorian desserts captivate the senses with their rich variety and the unique use of local ingredients, embodying the sweetness of Ecuador's vast biodiversity. These treats range from fruit-based delicacies, taking advantage of the country's abundant tropical fruits, to sugary confections that incorporate native grains and legumes. The creativity in dessert preparation in Ecuador showcases not only the culinary skills of its people but also their deep connection to the land, differentiating these sweet dishes from those of other cuisines with their distinct flavors and textures.

The flexibility of Ecuadorian desserts is demonstrated through their ability to blend traditional elements with modern influences, creating a wide spectrum of tastes that cater to all preferences. This versatility is key to their role in Ecuadorian cuisine, allowing for the exploration of new flavors while maintaining a link to cultural heritage. Additionally, many of these desserts offer nutritional benefits, incorporating ingredients like quinoa and amaranth, which are high in protein and minerals.

Thus, Ecuadorian desserts stand as a testament to the country's rich culinary tradition, offering both a treat to the palate and a reflection of its cultural diversity. Their delightful variety and the nutritional value they can offer make them an essential part of the gastronomic experience, celebrating Ecuador's commitment to flavor and health.

DULCE DE HIGOS CON QUESO

Ingredients

- Figs - 1 lb, stemmed.
- Sugar - 1 cup.
- Water - 4 cups.
- Cinnamon stick - 1.
- Cloves - 4.
- Fresh cheese (queso fresco) - for serving.

Instructions

1. In a large pot, combine the figs, sugar, water, cinnamon stick, and cloves. Bring to a boil over medium heat.

2. Reduce the heat to low and simmer for about 1 hour, or until the figs are soft and the syrup has thickened.

3. Remove from heat and let cool. The figs will continue to absorb the syrup as they cool.

4. Serve the figs with a slice of fresh cheese on the side.

HELADOS DE PAILA

Ingredients

- Fruit pulp (such as passion fruit, blackberry, or strawberry) - 2 cups.
- Sugar - 1 cup, or to taste.
- Water - 1 cup.
- Lemon juice - 2 tablespoons.

Instructions

1. In a saucepan, mix the fruit pulp, sugar, and water. Cook over medium heat until the sugar has dissolved.

2. Remove from heat and add the lemon juice. Mix well.

3. Allow the mixture to cool, then pour it into a shallow metal pan.

4. Place the pan in the freezer. Stir and scrape the mixture with a fork every 30 minutes to break up ice crystals, until it reaches a granita-like texture.

5. Serve in bowls or cups, optionally garnished with fresh fruit.

ESPUMILLAS

Ingredients

- Egg whites - 3.
- Guava pulp - 1 cup.
- Sugar - 1 cup.
- Lemon juice - 1 teaspoon.

Instructions

1. In a mixing bowl, beat the egg whites until stiff peaks form.

2. Gradually add the sugar while continuing to beat.

3. Add the guava pulp and lemon juice, and mix until well combined.

4. Pipe the mixture into small cups or onto a baking sheet lined with parchment paper.

5. Let the espumillas set at room temperature for a few hours until they are firm to the touch.

6. Serve as a light and fluffy dessert.

TRES LECHES

Ingredients

- Flour - 1 1/2 cups.
- Sugar - 1 cup.
- Eggs - 5.
- Milk - 1 cup.
- Evaporated milk - 1 can (12 oz).
- Sweetened condensed milk - 1 can (14 oz).
- Heavy cream - 1 cup.
- Vanilla extract - 1 teaspoon.
- Baking powder - 1 1/2 teaspoons.
- Salt - 1/2 teaspoon.

Instructions

1. Preheat the oven to 350°F (175°C). Grease and flour a 9x13 inch baking pan.

2. In a large bowl, sift together the flour, baking powder, and salt.

3. In another bowl, beat the eggs and 3/4 cup sugar until light and fluffy. Gradually add the flour mixture, mixing gently until combined.

4. Pour the batter into the prepared pan and bake for 25-30 minutes, or until a toothpick inserted into the center comes out clean.

5. Let the cake cool completely, then poke holes all over it

with a fork.

6. Mix the milk, evaporated milk, condensed milk, and vanilla extract. Pour the mixture over the cooled cake, allowing it to soak in.

7. Whip the heavy cream with the remaining sugar until stiff peaks form. Spread over the soaked cake.

8. Refrigerate for at least 4 hours before serving. Serve chilled.

BIZCOCHUELO

Ingredients

- Flour - 2 cups.
- Sugar - 1 cup.
- Eggs - 4.
- Baking powder - 2 teaspoons.
- Vanilla extract - 1 teaspoon.
- Milk - 1/2 cup.
- Butter - 1/4 cup, melted.

Instructions

1. Preheat the oven to 350°F (175°C). Grease and flour a round cake pan.

2. In a large bowl, beat the eggs and sugar until thick and pale, about 5 minutes.

3. Gradually add the flour and baking powder, mixing just until incorporated.

4. Stir in the vanilla extract, milk, and melted butter until the batter is smooth.

5. Pour the batter into the prepared pan and bake for 30-35 minutes, or until a toothpick inserted into the center comes out clean.

6. Let the cake cool in the pan for 10 minutes, then turn out onto a wire rack to cool completely.

7. Serve as is or decorate as desired. Bizcochuelo can be enjoyed plain, dusted with powdered sugar, or used as a base for layered cakes.

MOROCHO DULCE

Ingredients

- Morocho corn - 1 cup, soaked overnight.
- Milk - 4 cups.
- Cinnamon stick - 1.
- Cloves - 3.
- Sugar - 3/4 cup.
- Raisins - 1/2 cup.
- Ground cinnamon - 1/2 teaspoon.
- Shredded coconut - 1/4 cup (optional).

Instructions

1. Rinse the soaked morocho corn and drain well.

2. In a large pot, combine the morocho corn, milk, cinnamon stick, and cloves. Cook over medium heat, stirring frequently, until the mixture thickens, about 1 hour.

3. Add the sugar, raisins, and ground cinnamon. Continue cooking, stirring constantly, for another 15-20 minutes.

4. Remove the cinnamon stick and cloves. Serve the morocho warm, garnished with shredded coconut if desired.

LECHE ASADA

Ingredients

- Whole milk - 4 cups.
- Eggs - 4.
- Sugar - 3/4 cup.
- Vanilla extract - 1 teaspoon.
- Ground cinnamon - for sprinkling.

Instructions

1. Preheat the oven to 350°F (175°C).

2. In a bowl, whisk together the eggs, sugar, and vanilla extract until well combined. Gradually whisk in the milk.

3. Pour the mixture into a baking dish. Sprinkle the top lightly with ground cinnamon.

4. Place the baking dish in a larger pan and add hot water to the larger pan to come halfway up the sides of the baking dish.

5. Bake for 45-50 minutes, or until set and golden on top.

6. Allow to cool before serving. Leche asada can be served at room temperature or chilled.

ALFAJORES

Ingredients

- Flour - 2 cups.
- Cornstarch - 1 cup.
- Baking powder - 1 teaspoon.
- Salt - 1/2 teaspoon.
- Butter - 1 cup, softened.
- Confectioners' sugar - 3/4 cup.
- Egg yolks - 4.
- Lemon zest - 1 teaspoon.
- Dulce de leche - for filling.
- Coconut flakes - for coating.

Instructions

1. Sift together the flour, cornstarch, baking powder, and salt. Set aside.

2. In another bowl, cream the butter and confectioners' sugar until light and fluffy. Beat in the egg yolks and lemon zest.

3. Gradually mix in the dry ingredients to form a soft dough. Chill for 30 minutes.

4. On a floured surface, roll out the dough to about 1/8 inch thickness. Cut out rounds with a cookie cutter.

5. Place on baking sheets and bake at 350°F (175°C) for 10-12 minutes or until lightly golden. Let cool on wire racks.

6. Spread dulce de leche on half of the cookies and top with another cookie. Press the edges in coconut flakes.

7. Serve the alfajores as a sweet treat at any time of the day.

BUÑUELOS

Ingredients

- All-purpose flour - 2 cups.
- Baking powder - 1 teaspoon.
- Salt - 1/2 teaspoon.
- Sugar - 2 tablespoons.
- Eggs - 2.
- Milk - 3/4 cup.
- Vanilla extract - 1 teaspoon.
- Vegetable oil - for frying.
- Cinnamon sugar - for coating.

Instructions

1. In a large bowl, mix together the flour, baking powder, salt, and sugar.

2. Beat in the eggs, milk, and vanilla until a smooth batter forms.

3. Heat oil in a deep fryer or large pan to 375°F (190°C).

4. Drop spoonfuls of batter into the hot oil and fry until golden brown on all sides.

5. Remove with a slotted spoon and drain on paper towels.

6. Roll the warm buñuelos in cinnamon sugar to coat.

7. Serve warm for a delicious dessert or snack.

QUESADILLAS ECUATORIANAS

Ingredients

- Flour - 3 cups.
- Baking powder - 1 teaspoon.
- Salt - 1/2 teaspoon.
- Butter - 1 cup, softened.
- Sugar - 1 cup.
- Eggs - 3.
- Grated cheese (queso fresco or mozzarella) - 1 cup.
- Milk - 1/2 cup.

Instructions

1. Preheat the oven to 375°F (190°C) and grease a baking sheet.

2. In a bowl, sift together the flour, baking powder, and salt.

3. In another bowl, cream the butter and sugar until light and fluffy. Add the eggs one at a time, beating well after each addition.

4. Gradually add the dry ingredients to the butter mixture, alternating with the milk.

5. Stir in the grated cheese until just combined.

6. Drop spoonfuls of the batter onto the prepared baking sheet.

7. Bake for 15-20 minutes, or until golden brown and a toothpick inserted into the center comes out clean.

8. Serve warm or at room temperature. Enjoy these sweet

and cheesy quesadillas as a dessert or a snack.

ARROZ CON LECHE

Ingredients

- Rice - 1 cup.
- Water - 2 cups.
- Cinnamon stick - 1.
- Whole milk - 4 cups.
- Sugar - 1 cup.
- Raisins - 1/2 cup (optional).
- Ground cinnamon - for garnish.

Instructions

1. In a large pot, bring the water to a boil. Add the rice and cinnamon stick. Reduce heat to low and cook until the water is absorbed.

2. Add the milk and sugar to the pot. Simmer over low heat, stirring frequently, until the rice is tender and the mixture has thickened, about 25-30 minutes.

3. Remove from heat and remove the cinnamon stick. Stir in the raisins if using.

4. Serve warm or cold, garnished with ground cinnamon.

FLAN DE COCO

Ingredients

- Coconut milk - 1 can (13.5 oz).
- Eggs - 3.
- Condensed milk - 1 can (14 oz).
- Vanilla extract - 1 teaspoon.

- Sugar - 3/4 cup (for caramel).

Instructions

1. Preheat the oven to 350°F (175°C). Place sugar in a medium saucepan over medium heat. Cook until the sugar melts and becomes golden. Pour the caramel into a round baking dish, swirling to coat the bottom.

2. In a blender, combine the coconut milk, eggs, condensed milk, and vanilla extract. Blend until smooth.

3. Pour the mixture over the caramel in the baking dish. Place the dish in a larger baking pan and add hot water to the outer pan to come halfway up the sides of the dish.

4. Bake in the preheated oven for about 1 hour or until set.

5. Let cool, then refrigerate until cold. To serve, run a knife around the edges of the flan and invert onto a plate.

PRISTIÑOS

Ingredients

- All-purpose flour - 2 cups.
- Sugar - 1 tablespoon.
- Butter - 1/4 cup, melted.
- Orange juice - 1/2 cup.
- Anise seeds - 1 teaspoon.
- Salt - 1/2 teaspoon.
- Vegetable oil - for frying.
- Panela or brown sugar syrup - for serving.

Instructions

1. In a large bowl, mix the flour, sugar, melted butter, orange juice, anise seeds, and salt to form a dough. Knead until smooth.

2. Roll out the dough on a floured surface to about 1/4 inch thickness. Cut into strips and twist each strip into a pretzel shape.

3. Heat the oil in a deep fryer or large pan. Fry the pristiños until golden brown. Drain on paper towels.

4. Serve warm, drizzled with panela or brown sugar syrup.

EMPANADAS DE VIENTO DULCES

Ingredients

- All-purpose flour - 2 cups.
- Sugar - 1/2 cup (for dough), extra for sprinkling.
- Butter - 1/4 cup, cold and cubed.
- Egg - 1.
- Water - as needed.
- Filling of choice (sweet cheese, guava paste, etc.) - 1/2 cup.
- Oil - for frying.

Instructions

1. In a bowl, combine the flour and 1/2 cup sugar. Add the cubed butter and work it into the flour with your fingers until the mixture resembles coarse crumbs.

2. Stir in the egg and add enough water to form a smooth dough. Knead briefly, then let rest for 30 minutes.

3. Roll out the dough on a floured surface and cut into rounds. Place a small amount of filling in the center of each round.

4. Fold the dough over the filling to create a half-moon shape. Press the edges to seal.

5. Heat the oil in a deep fryer or large pan. Fry the empanadas until golden brown. Drain on paper towels.

6. Sprinkle with sugar while still warm. Serve as a delicious sweet treat.

BOCADITOS DE CALABAZA

Ingredients

- Pumpkin - 2 cups, cooked and mashed.
- Sugar - 1 cup.
- Egg - 1.
- All-purpose flour - 2 cups.
- Baking powder - 1 teaspoon.
- Cinnamon - 1/2 teaspoon.
- Nutmeg - 1/4 teaspoon.
- Salt - 1/2 teaspoon.
- Butter - 1/4 cup, melted.

Instructions

1. Preheat the oven to 350°F (175°C) and line a baking sheet with parchment paper.

2. In a large bowl, mix the cooked pumpkin, sugar, and egg until well combined.

3. In another bowl, sift together the flour, baking powder, cinnamon, nutmeg, and salt.

4. Gradually add the dry ingredients to the pumpkin mixture, mixing until just combined. Stir in the melted butter.

5. Drop spoonfuls of the batter onto the prepared baking sheet.

6. Bake for 15-20 minutes, or until lightly golden. Allow to cool on a wire rack.

7. Serve the bocaditos de calabaza as a delightful dessert or snack.

RECIPE LIST

BREAKFASTS

BOLÓN DE VERDE 9
TIGRILLO 10
MOTE PILLO 11
EMPANADAS DE VIENTO 11
LLAPINGACHOS 12
CEVICHE DE CAMARÓN (BREAKFAST VERSION) 13
HUMITAS 13
QUIMBOLITOS 14
PAN DE YUCA 15
YAPINGACHOS 15
ENCEBOLLADO 16
TAMAL DE MAÍZ 17
MOROCHO 17
CHUCULA 18
AREPAS ECUATORIANAS 19

SOUPS

LOCRO DE PAPA 20
SOPA DE BOLAS DE VERDE 21
CALDO DE PATAS 22
SOPA DE QUINUA 23
AGUADO DE GALLINA 24
SOPA DE LENTEJAS 25

CALDO DE BOLAS DE VERDE 26
SOPA DE FIDEOS 27
MENESTRA DE LENTEJAS.. 27
CHUPE DE PESCADO 28
SOPA DE GUANDÚ 29
CREMA DE ACHOJCHA 30
SOPA DE ZAPALLO 31
CALDO DE 31 31
SOPA DE POLLO CON NOODLES DE PAPA 32
SOPA DE GUANDÚ 33
CREMA DE ACHOJCHA 34
SOPA DE ZAPALLO 35
CALDO DE 31 35
SOPA DE POLLO CON NOODLES DE PAPA 36

BROTHS
CALDO DE PATA 38
CALDO DE MANGUERA 39
CALDO DE GALLINA CRIOLLA 40
YAGUARLOCRO 41
CALDO DE BAGRE.. 42
CALDO DE SALCHICHA 42
AGUADO DE GALLINA 43
CALDO DE GUAGUAS 44
CALDO DE CUERO 44
CONSOMÉ DE POLLO 45

CALDO DE PEZ VELA 46

CALDO DE COSTILLA...47

CALDO TLALPEÑO ECUATORIANO............................47

CALDO DE HUESO DE RES 48

CALDO DE CAMARÓN..49

SEAFOOD DISHES

CEVICHE DE CAMARÓN 50

ENCOCADO DE PESCADO 51

CEVICHE DE PESCADO 52

CORVICHE 53

ENCEBOLLADO...54

CEVICHE DE CONCHA..54

CAZUELA DE MARISCOS 55

CEVICHE DE LANGOSTINOS..56

PESCADO ENCOCADO 57

SUDADO DE PESCADO 58

CEVICHE DE CALAMAR 59

CEVICHE DE PULPO 59

ARROZ MARINERO..60

SOPA MARINERA...61

CAMARONES AL AJILLO 62

BEEF DISHES

LOMO SALTADO..64

SECO DE CARNE 65

FRITADA 66
CARNE COLORADA 67
ESTOFADO DE CARNE 67
HORNADO 68
GUATITA 69
ASADO DE RES 70
BISTEC DE PALOMILLA 71
CARNE EN PALITO 72
LENGUA EN SALSA DE MANÍ 72
COSTILLAS BBQ ESTILO ECUATORIANO 73
ROLLO DE CARNE RELLENO 74
CHURRASCO ECUATORIANO 75
ALBÓNDIGAS ECUATORIANAS 76

PORK DISHES
HORNADO ECUATORIANO 77
FRITADA DE CHANCHO 78
SECO DE CHIVO 79
LLAPINGACHOS CON CHORIZO 80
CHICHARRONES 80
MOTE CON CHICHARRÓN 81
TAMALES DE CHANCHO 82
EMPANADAS DE MOROCHO, CARNE DE CERDO 83
GUATITA 83
COSTILLAS DE CERDO EN SALSA DE TAMARINDO 84
CHANCHO AL HORNO 85

CARNE AHUMADA 86
LECHÓN ASADO 87
MORCILLAS 88
PERNIL AL HORNO 88

CHICKEN DISHES
AJÍ DE GALLINA 91
SECO DE POLLO 92
ARROZ CON POLLO 92
CALDO DE GALLINA 93
POLLO AL HORNO CON SALSA DE NARANJA 94
ENCOCADO DE POLLO 95
POLLO A LA BRASA 96
GUISO DE POLLO 97
POLLO SUDADO 98
CUY ASADO 98
ESTOFADO DE POLLO 99
MENESTRA DE POLLO 100
POLLO CON MIEL Y MOSTAZA 101
POLLO RELLENO 102
GALLINA CUYANA 103

VEGETARIAN DISHES
QUINOA CON CHAMPIÑONES 106
LOCRO DE ZAPALLO 107
CEVICHE DE PALMITO 107

ENSALADA DE QUINUA 108
TORTILLAS DE MAÍZ CON QUESO 109
MOTE SUCIO 110
ENSALADA ECUATORIANA 111
CHOCLO CON QUESO 111
TOSTADAS CON AGUACATE 112
EMPANADAS DE VERDE 113
PATACONES CON AJO 113
LENTEJAS ESTOFADAS 114
ARROZ CON MENESTRA 115
HUMITAS DE CHOCLO 116
PASTEL DE CHOCLO 117

RICE DISHES
ARROZ CON CAMARÓN 119
ARROZ CON POLLO 120
ARROZ CON MENESTRA Y CARNE ASADA 121
ARROZ MARINERO 122
ARROZ CON CALAMARES 123
ARROZ CON CHORIZO 124
ARROZ CON COCO 125
ARROZ CON GUANDULES 125
ARROZ TÍPICO ECUATORIANO 126
RISOTTO DE QUINOA 127
ARROZ VERDE 128
ARROZ CON CHAMPIÑONES 129

ARROZ CON PATO 130
ARROZ CON LECHE (DESSERT VERSION) 131
ARROZ NEGRO 131

SAUCES

AJI CRIOLLO 133
SALSA DE MANÍ 134
SALSA VERDE 135
SALSA DE TOMATE CRIOLLA 136
CHIMICHURRI ECUATORIANO 136
SALSA ROSADA 137
SALSA DE AJO 138
SALSA DE CILANTRO 138
ENCURTIDO (PICKLED ONIONS AND TOMATOES) 139
SALSA DE TAMARINDO 140

BREADS

PAN DE YUCA 142
PAN DE MAÍZ 143
PAN DE QUESO 144
ROSCAS 145
BIZCOCHOS DE CAYAMBE 146
PAN DE ALMIDÓN 147
GUAGUAS DE PAN 148
PAN DE PINLLO 149
TORTILLAS DE TRIGO 150

BOLLOS DE MAÍZ 151

DESSERTS
DULCE DE HIGOS CON QUESO................................ 153
HELADOS DE PAILA 153
ESPUMILLAS... 154
TRES LECHES 155
BIZCOCHUELO 156
MOROCHO DULCE 157
LECHE ASADA 158
ALFAJORES 159
BUÑUELOS 160
QUESADILLAS ECUATORIANAS.............................. 161
ARROZ CON LECHE... 162
FLAN DE COCO 162
PRISTIÑOS 163
EMPANADAS DE VIENTO DULCES 164
BOCADITOS DE CALABAZA 165

Printed in Dunstable, United Kingdom